MW00476404

)

Other books by Deng Ming-Dao

The Chronicles of Tao
    The Wandering Taoist
    Seven Bamboo Tablets of the Cloudy Satchel
    Gateway to a Vast World

Scholar Warrior

365 Tao

Everyday Tao

Zen: The Art of Modern Eastern Cooking

The Living I Ching

The Lunar Tao

The Wisdom
of the Tao

Ancient Stories That
Delight, Inform, and Inspire

SELECTED AND EDITED BY

Deng Ming-Dao

author of *365 Tao*

Cover design by Deng Ming-Dao

Cover art: *Clearing After Rain Over Streams and Mountains,* by Wang Hui (Chinese, Qing dynasty, 1662) Hanging scroll; ink on paper. The Metropolitan Museum of Art, Bequest of John M. Crawford Jr., 1988

Interior image by Deng Ming-Dao, based on *Night-Shining White,* by Han Gan, The Metropolitan Museum of Art.

Interior design and typsettting by Side By Side Studios, San Francisco, CA

Hampton Roads Publishing Company, Inc.
Charlottesville, VA 22906
Distributed by Red Wheel/Weiser, LLC
WWW.REDWHEELWEISER.COM

SIGN UP FOR OUR NEWSLETTER AND SPECIAL OFFERS BY GOING TO *WWW.REDWHEELWEISER.COM/NEWSLETTER.*

ISBN: 978-1-57174-837-9

Library of Congress Control Number: 2017958286

Printed in Canada

MAR
10 9 8 7 6 5 4 3 2 1

Contents

Introduction

Imagine old-time China when people heard their news and tales from wandering storytellers. In the villages, these chroniclers might have shouted for people to gather under a shady tree. In the cities, they might have banged on a cymbal to attract people moving through parks or marketplaces. They were the journalists, entertainers, dramatists, and comedians of their day, and they jostled for attention among acrobats, fortune-tellers, bards, minstrels, commentators, healers, and mendicants. Whoever was the most exciting, the most informative, and the most intriguing was the winner who drew the largest crowds. Imagine, then, these people coming to your town, stirring up the sleepy populace, fascinating listeners with stories both familiar and novel, and perhaps even inspiring a few to run away to find adventure.

All the stories in this book are thousands of years old. They had to be special to last through years of telling and retelling, and they were compelling enough for visitors to carry them beyond the borders of China, to translate them, and to retell them in other lands. They expressed great wisdom by fusing anecdote with philosophy. The stories are frequently humorous, ribald, irreverent, pithy, or sarcastic—but they always speak to great and universal truths.

Their form often took on the guise of tall tales—distances and measurements were highly exaggerated, time was indistinct (the better to put us in an eternal present), historical personages were made into tropes or used for poking fun, fictional characters were thrown in willy-nilly, and an age of legendary kings was invoked as a utopian ideal—even though those centuries were already in the distant past when these anecdotes were first told. (In this book, you can tell when a person was real by dates given in parentheses at their first mention.)

These stories were recorded in scattered writings, but it's apparent that those texts were scaffolds for further telling. The ideas continued to evolve over long periods. They were not organized into static persuasive texts but remained a seemingly random jumble of themes. They borrow similar formats from one another, sometimes reworking themes from different angles and reinforcing the idea that these tales were meant for improvisation, adaptation, and variation. The stories were passed on as people needed them, their wording meandered creatively, and they were embellished to this day as storytelling was always meant to do.

This process was augmented by how learning developed in the ancient tradition: the teachers insisted on memorization and experience over the written word. Many of these stories originate from the era of The Hundred Schools of Thought (sixth century–221 BCE), a time that ended when the First Emperor grew frustrated at the many arguments of bickering scholars and ordered most of the books in the empire burned. The Emperor Wenzong (r. 827–840) of the Tang Dynasty made a valiant attempt at standardization by ordering twelve classics carved into the front and back of 114 massive stone slabs and installed in public so that no one could ever argue about versions again. But those steles stood in one place—the Imperial College in Chang'an (now Xi'an). The country was vast. A large number of individual teachers continued to wander the roads and sail the rivers looking for pupils or, in emulation of their greatest example, Confucius, who sought the patronage of an emperor, duke, or at least a rich merchant family with whom they would live. The storytellers went everywhere too, with more itinerant goals, but with similar messages.

As a result, the stories evolved into myths. They became the essential distillation of shared wisdom and vital gifts to anyone who heard them. Each generation adapted them and found fresh understanding in them. Accordingly, the stories in this book have been edited and their language has been updated. If you're curious about the sources, initials in parentheses and a key at the end of the book provide identification.

In imperial times, it was seldom safe to criticize officials, let alone the king or emperor. But these stories don't shy away from that, holding the rich and powerful up to ridicule and satirizing the very logic, morality, history, and rhetoric that had been carved into stone.

The storytellers took the dry format of dialogue between a master teacher and student, debates between philosophers, or the interchanges between minister and ruler and inflated them wildly. The point was unabashedly political: turn away from pomposity and corruption, remember the common people, share generously, and be aware of the pitfalls of being king. These stories speak truth to power. That helps us, because each generation wrestles with the same questions of inequality, justice, and social good.

When I was a boy, I didn't get specific lessons on how to live. I got stories. If I asked why I had to believe some concept, a person such as my grandmother might reply with, "This is true because of what happened to the Yellow Emperor," and then the story would follow. What intrigues me is that this habit hasn't changed even after China's revolution, rapid modernization, digital technology, and global culture. People still say, "It's true because . . ." before they invoke a story that is more than two thousand years old.

We need stories. They help us make sense of who we are and how we got here. They keep us sane as we try to absorb our experiences, our aging, and our thoughts. We want to know that we're living in a way that measures up, and we do that by comparing ourselves to stories. We tell stories to children to prepare them for the world. Stories help us visualize the future by taking the messages of yesterday and helping us get tomorrow right.

The stories collected in this book speak to two important emotions: fear and love. Repeatedly, fear is identified as the greatest threat. Even death is acceptable, as it must be, but fear is shown to be the more troublesome of the two. We need not fear as long as we gain insight into ourselves and we understand that we are part of nature and connected to one another. We are urged to turn away from indigence and instead seek clarity of character. At the same time, love is held up as one of the greatest qualities of life. We are urged to love all of existence, to see ourselves on a par with all creatures, to show kindness to others, to love ourselves even if that means others might consider us ugly or "useless," and to embrace love as the most honest truth of the heart.

The majority of these stories are taken from two Taoist sources, Zhuangzi (370–287 BCE) and Liezi (c. fifth century BCE). We don't know much about either author. That ambiguity would delight them both, because they would have said that it was not the person that mattered but rather the lessons. Both books belong to the Taoist Canon, a collection of about 1, 400 texts.

The word *Tao* appears frequently in these texts. Just as the storytellers wrapped great truths in legendary tales, the word *Tao* was used in contexts from the mundane to the extraordinary. *Tao* means a road, a way, a method, a principle, or a truth. It might be appended to the name of a thoroughfare, and it can just as easily indicate all the cosmos. The fact that the word has so many different meanings shows that it runs through every part of life. It's completely consistent that the word is used for the names of bars, in jokes, or even in the teenage slang of today. Tao is that flexible because it is part of everything, from daily banter to sacred song.

The ideograph for Tao (pinyin: *dao*) combines a picture of a head with the symbol for walking. Tao is a person on a path. By extension, everything in the universe has a path. Everything moves and proceeds in its own natural way. The essence of a good life is to match one's personal way with the universal way. You might see yourself as that person on the path, pausing in your travel to hear a new story, and passing your own on to others.

Taoism is China's indigenous spiritual tradition. That's why some of these stories refer to the beginnings of Chinese civilization, to the times of the legendary emperors such as the Yellow Emperor and Emperor Yao. When these stories begin with a reference to ancient times, it tells us that we are a part of a long continuum of those who contemplated existence. We are each unique and yet we face the same choices as those who lived before us.

These remarkable wisdom-stories combine spirituality, philosophy, cosmology, governance, observations of the human condition, frank talk about life and death, and the eternal continuity of this marvelous word. They urge us to be simple, plain, and honest. Contentment, kindness, independence, understanding, and gratitude are all that we need. In telling us about people from all eras and roles in life, the storytellers urge us to be grateful, for we receive every benefit from this world.

Tao is a journey. Whether we live in one place all our lives or whether we are fortunate enough to travel all over this globe, we each go through our own life's journey. We are part of a grand procession, finding our place in our area, our time, and in history. In these stories, the world is called heaven and earth and that's exactly where we travel. Heaven and earth are both time and place; they provide the pace and setting for our entire lives. We need do nothing more than move to that rhythm. Our lives form our story: they tell our Tao.

1 | Fishing for Something Big

Prince Ren got a huge iron hook, a thick black silk line, a bamboo pole, and fifty steers for bait. He squatted on Kuaiji Mountain and cast his line into the far-off East Ocean. The prince fished every morning for an entire year, but didn't catch anything.

Finally, a monstrous fish gobbled the bait. It dived, dragging hook and line behind it. Then it burst to the surface, beating its fins, frothing the waters, and raising mountainous white waves. The whole sea shook and the noise was like demons fighting gods. People were terrified for a thousand kilometers around.

The prince finally landed the fish, cut the body into pieces, and dried them. Crowds came from far away in the east and north to eat their fill.

For generations since, roaming storytellers have repeated this tale as they tried to outdo one another. They never mention this: what if Prince Ren had held his rod and line over ditches and had just tried to catch minnows? Would he have caught such a big fish?

Likewise, those who dress up small fables to get a position for themselves are not of wide intelligence—just as anyone who doesn't know the story of Prince Ren really isn't able to lead the world. (Z)

2 | The Superlative Horse

Duke Mu of Qin said to Bo Le, his best judge of horses: "You are growing old. Could I ask your sons to find horses for me in your place?"

Bo Le replied: "Anyone can find an excellent horse by looking at its build, its color, its muscles, and its bone structure. But only a rare few can find a superlative horse that raises no dust and leaves no tracks. Although my sons have the talent to find excellent horses, they cannot see a superlative horse. However, I do have a friend named Gao who is a firewood and vegetable hawker. His ability to choose horses is as good as mine. Please talk to him."

So Duke Mu summoned Gao and hired him to look for horses. Gao returned after three months and reported that he had found a horse in Shaqiu.

The duke asked him eagerly: "What kind of horse is it?"

Gao replied, "It is a brown mare."

Duke Mu sent for the horse with great excitement. But he was disappointed weeks later when the grooms brought him a black stallion.

The duke was speechless with anger and summoned Bo Le. "This is terrible. The man you recommended doesn't know the difference between colors or whether a horse is a stallion or a mare! How can he possibly judge horses?"

Bo Le sighed deeply. "Has he progressed that far? Then he's worth a million of me and there is no comparing us. His vision is superior! He sees the divine workings and the subtle essence instead of coarse appearances. He sees what's inside and is not fooled by what's outside. He sees what ought to be seen and ignores what ought to be ignored. Gao can truly judge horses!"

Bo Le asked to see the steed. When it was led in, he saw right away that it was a superlative horse. (L)

3 | Between Small and Large

King Tang (c. 1675–1646 BCE) said to Minister Ji: "A vast dark ocean in the barren north is called the Pool of Heaven. A fish several hundred kilometers wide and of a-length-no-one-has-ever-seen lives there.

"Similarly, a bird named the *peng* has a back as large as the sacred mountain Tai and wings that spread through the sky like clouds. When it soars into the heavens, its path of flight spirals like the whorls of a goat's horn. After rising some twenty kilometers through the cloudy air and looking as if it could lift the whole blue sky, it then sets its course for the distant south."

Overhearing this, a quail on the bank of a marsh laughed and said, "Where could such a bird be going? I can spring up and land in just a few yards. I can dart between raspberry bushes and mugwort and I'm done with my flight. Where could such a creature possibly need to go?"

Such are the differences between the small and large. In the same way, some people might know enough to hold office, or to be the head of a village, or to serve a ruler and help guide a state—but they are as shortsighted as that quail. (Z)

4 | The Sage Has No Thought of Fame

There was once a great person named Song Rongzi. He was like this: If the whole world had praised him, he would not have been flattered. If the whole world had condemned him, he would not have been discouraged.

He clearly knew the difference between inner and outer and the difference between glory and disgrace. However, that was as far as he went. He could account for everything, but he couldn't fully find his own place in the world.

Or take Liezi as another example. He could ride the wind skillfully and smoothly, but he couldn't stay up in the sky forever. He had to come down after fifteen days. Liezi was not a scheming person. He didn't grab for what everybody else calls happiness, and he didn't even need to travel like other people—but there were still times when he had to wait for the right conditions so that he could fly again.

However, what if you could mount the truth of heaven and earth and ride on the variations of the Six Energies? You could roam without limits!

Therefore, it is said: A realized person gives no thought to self. A spiritual person gives no thought to their own merit. A sage gives no thought to fame. (Z)

5

5 | Failing to Distinguish What's Real

There was once a man from the eastern territories who was named Yuan Jingmu. He was on a journey and one day collapsed from hunger while he was walking. A robber named Qiu saw him lying by the side of the road and brought him a bowl of food.

After swallowing three mouthfuls, Yuan Jingmu feebly opened his eyes and asked: "Who are you?"

"I am a native of Hu Fu. My name is Qiu."

Yuan Jingmu screamed. "Aren't you the wicked robber of Hu Fu? Why are you feeding me? I am a good man and will not eat your food!"

He dug his hands into the ground and tried to throw up. Nothing came out. He tried again several more times, crawled into a ditch, and died.

Now, the robber from Hu Fu might have been a bad man, but there was nothing wrong with his food. If you won't eat his food because you think it's sinful, then you have lost all reason. (L)

6 | Reason for Song

Confucius was traveling through a big mountain range when he came across an old man sitting alone in the wilderness. He was clothed in deerskin, had a rope for a belt, and strummed a zither as he sang.

Confucius said: "Sir, you play such heartfelt music!"

"My music is great and varied," replied the man, "because heaven birthed the ten thousand things and gave us great riches. Heaven gives me all the benefits of life. That's the first reason I sing.

"Man and woman are distinct and different. A man must be respectful and a woman modest, and this adds to my wealth. I have both done and received what a man should. That's the second reason I sing.

"Some newborns will never see the sun or moon, and others will never grow out of their swaddling clothes. But I have already walked the earth for ninety years. That's the third reason I sing.

"Poverty is the lot of the scholar, death is everyone's end. I dwell in the absolute and am pleased overall. Why should I worry?"

"Excellent!" Confucius said. "Here's someone who is wise in his own lot." (L)

7 | Covering Eyes with a Leaf

A poor man once read that praying mantises hid behind certain leaves to catch cicadas and that if human beings could find these leaves it would make them invisible. So he decided to find these marvelous leaves.

He went out and swept up a bunch of leaves and brought them home to test. One by one, he held a leaf in front of his face and asked his wife whether she could see him.

"Yes I can," she said each time. This went on for days, until she grew tired of being pestered and said, "I can't see you anymore."

Overjoyed, the man went to the marketplace, held the leaf in front of himself, and proceeded to steal whatever he could. Naturally, he was arrested right away.

The magistrate asked him: "Weren't you afraid of being caught?"

"No," said the man. "Once I held the leaf in front of my eyes, I couldn't see anything." (FL)

8 | Plowing for a Dog

There was once a man who loved hunting so much that he wasted all his days chasing animals. But he wasn't a good hunter and usually didn't catch anything. He grew ashamed to face his family, friends, and fellow villagers. He was sure that the reason he was a bad hunter was because he had a bad hunting dog. Although he wanted to buy a good dog, his family was too poor to afford one.

Eventually, he went back home and he threw himself into plowing. He worked so hard that his family became wealthy and he was finally able to afford a good dog. After that he was able to hunt and bring back more animals than anyone else.

From ancient times to now, no one has ever become a ruler without first plowing. This separates the worthy from the unworthy. When worthy leaders see an improper course, they won't follow it. When they see a proper course, they will pursue it. They follow the Tao and avoid harm. (LBW)

9 | The Foolish Old Man

Two mountains named Taixing and Wangwu together covered some 350 square kilometers and were each 20,000 meters high. They originally stood in southern Jizhou, north of the Yang River. The Foolish Old Man of North Mountain, who was already ninety years old, was annoyed because the two mountains blocked travelers from reaching the sea.

He called his family together to discuss the situation. They said: "We could use all our strength, level the mountains, and reach the ocean. What do you say?"

Everyone agreed except his wife, who was doubtful. "My dear husband, you don't even have the strength to sweep away a pile of dirt. How could you possibly move Taixing and Wangwu? Where would you even put the dirt and rock?"

The others broke in, "We will take all the earth and dump it off the shore of Bohai."

So the Foolish Old Man, his son, and his grandson went out with picks and began hewing away the rock, shoveling the soil, carrying dirt away in baskets, and dumping the debris at the shore. The son of a widow who lived nearby was so young he still had his milk teeth, but he got excited and jumped to help them. Together, they kept working and only went home once at the turn of each season.

The Wise Old Man of Riverbend laughed at them and told them to give up. "With the poor remaining strength of your advanced years, you will not succeed in moving even a hair's breadth of the mountains. How will you possibly move all that soil and rock?"

The Foolish Old Man let out a long sigh and said, "Your mind is so closed that I can hardly get through to you. You're not even a match for the widow's son with his slight strength. I may die, but my son will survive me. My son will raise grandchildren, and those grandchildren will have children of their own. My family will never end but the mountains cannot grow any taller. What difficulty, then, should it be to level them?" The Wise Old Man of Riverbend was speechless.

However, a nearby snake spirit was startled to hear their exchange. He rushed to report to the heavenly ruler who was moved by the old man's sincerity. He commanded two sons of the divine Kua'e Clan to carry the mountains away to the four directions. (L)

11

10 | The Jingwei Bird Tries to Fill the Sea

Far to the southeast stands Departing Doves Mountain. Mulberry trees cover its slopes.

A bird that looks like a crow with a decorated head, and that has a white beak and red feet, lives in those trees. It is called the Jingwei and it makes a sound like its name.

One day, the younger daughter of Nuwa was swimming in the Eastern Sea. She could not get back to shore and she drowned.

Her spirit turned into the Jingwei birds. For centuries since, these birds regularly carry twigs and stones from the Western Mountains to drop into the waters—trying to fill the Eastern Sea. (CMS)

11 | In the Great Beginning

In the great beginning was nothing. All was without name or form.

Then came a movement within formlessness, and that led to the birth of things that we could properly call real. What was formless separated and we can say that those distinctions led to order.

All things came from this process of melding and movement. Once everything became fully evident, there were patterns. Then we can finally say that all was present.

Form embodies a spirit—each thing has its attributes that we call its nature. Once its nature is refined, it returns to its proper character, a character that, once fully realized, is the same as the great beginning. It's identical to the void—a great and utter emptiness!

Heaven and earth join like a bird beak fitting closed. They are drawn together as if linked by a cord. It might seem hard to understand or it might seem confusing, but it is this profound mystery that we must obey and with which we must remain in accord. (Z)

13

12 | The Wind in the Hollows

Nanguo Ziqi sat leaning on an armrest with his head tilted toward the sky. Breathing gently, he seemed to be in a trance and unaware of anyone around him. His student, Yancheng Ziyou, stood before him in attendance, said, "What is this? Can a body become like a withered tree? Can the mind be as dead as ash? The one who leans on this armrest today is not like the one who leaned on the armrest yesterday."

Ziqi said to him: "Yan, you do well to ask such a question. I had just lost myself, but how can I explain that to you?

"You may have heard the piping of people, but you may not have heard the piping of the earth. You may have heard the piping of the earth, but you may not have heard the piping of heaven."

"May I dare ask you to explain?"

"When there's a great blast of air, it's called the wind. It comes and goes. When it appears, it howls through the many openings in nature. Have you heard its roaring? The mountain forests bend, the spaces between great trees with their trunks some hundred spans around become like nostrils. Or like mouths. Or ears. Or like crossings, or circles. Or like mortars, wet footprints, or big puddles. The sounds are like crashing waves, whizzing arrows—scolding, sucking, wheezing, crying, shouting, wailing, gnawing. They start with a hum and swell to a bellow.

"Gentle breezes produce small effects. Cyclonic winds produce big effects. Once the fierce gusts have passed, the countless openings are empty again. Have you seen such tossing and quivering?"

Yan said: "The piping of the earth may indeed come from the many openings. The piping of people comes from bamboo tubes. What about the notes of heaven?"

Ziqi said: "The many blowings are all different. They appear by themselves, they stop by themselves. Do we know who stirs them up?" (Z)

13 | The Right View

An expert on swords said: "White metal makes a sword hard, and yellow metal makes it sharp. Mix them and you will have both hard and sharp. That will be an excellent sword."

Someone disagreed with him: "White metal makes a sword soft, and yellow metal makes it dull. The blade will be neither hard nor sharp. A soft blade will bend, a dull one will snap. If both metals are mixed, how will you have a good sword?"

The ingredients of the sword were the same, and yet one person called them good and the other called them bad. That was what they were arguing about. Therefore, one should listen intelligently and avoid absurd discussions.

Without smart and careful listening, even the Emperors Yao (2358–2258 BCE) and Jie (1728–1675 BCE) couldn't tell the difference. This is what causes problems for loyal ministers and leads to the worthy ones being dismissed. (LBW)

14 | The Banquet

Mister Tian opened his ancestral hall and gave a lavish banquet for a thousand guests. They came with gifts of fish and wild game. As he sat among the crowd, Master Tian looked at the presents and sighed with satisfaction: "How great is heaven! It sprouts the five grains and breeds fish and fowl for us to use." All the guests applauded Mister Tian's wisdom.

But a twelve-year-old boy from the Bao family stood up and spoke without regard to rank or propriety: "The situation is not as our lord says. Heaven and earth bring forth all living beings to be in the same class as us. No being is greater or lesser than any other one. Due to size, strength, or cunning, it may be that some overpower and feed upon others, but none were born to be less than others.

"People may catch animals to eat, but should we say that heaven created animals for people? Mosquitoes and gnats bite us. Tigers and wolves sometimes attack and eat people. But that does not mean that heaven created humans for mosquitoes and gnats to bite or to give flesh to tigers and wolves."
(L)

17

15 | The Lost Horse

A man named Sai Weng lived on the northern frontier. One day, his mare ran across the border into nomad territory. His neighbors came to offer their sympathies, but Sai Weng's father said, "What makes you sure this isn't a blessing?"

Some months later the horse returned, bringing a splendid nomad stallion with it. The neighbors came to offer their congratulations, but Sai Weng's father said, "What makes you sure this isn't a disaster?"

Their household was now richer by a fine horse, which Sai Weng loved to ride. One day, though, Sai Weng fell and broke his hip. His neighbors came to console him, but Sai Weng's father said, "What makes you sure this isn't a blessing?"

A year later, a massive force of nomads crossed the border and every able-bodied man grabbed his bow and arrows to go into battle. Sai Weng was exempt because he was disabled. The village lost nine of every ten men. Only because Sai Weng was lame did father and son survive to take care of each other.

Truly, blessing turns to disaster, and disaster to blessing: the changes have no end, nor can the mystery be fathomed. (FT)

16 | You'll Know in Time

Yu Xiong said: "The movement of this world never stops. But who can perceive the secret process of heaven and earth? Things that are reduced here are enlarged there; things that are produced there are destroyed here. Reduction and enlargement, growth and decay—these are the constants in life and death. These stages come and go, one after another, never missing a step.

"How can we begin to know of this? All is of one energy, progressing without pause, and yet all forms suffer unavoidable decay. Most of us don't notice completion any more than we notice decay.

"Likewise, from birth to death, people change in appearance, color, mentality, and capability every day. Skin, nails, and hair begin to grow at birth, and then fall apart in old age. From infancy on, we cannot halt this process of change.

"We may remain unaware of it in our earlier years. But just wait until old age arrives and you'll know in time." (L)

17 | How the World Began

The ancient sages said that heaven and earth were controlled by yin and yang, and that form came from the formless. So where did heaven and earth come from?

I explain it like this: "There was a great transformation. There was a great origin. There was a great beginning. There was a great root.

"Before the great transformation, there was no energy yet. Then came the great origin and the beginning of energy. That great beginning produced great form. That led to the great root—and the start of all matter.

"In the earliest states, energy, form, and matter were not yet separated from one another. We can say that all was murky and unclear.

"During that time when all was murky and unclear, everything that was yet to come was also mixed together and could not be separated from one another. They were seen but not seen, heard but not heard, swirling without resistance until further change came.

"Change has no form or limit. Change and transformation are one. A single change leads to seven. A change of seven leads to nine. Investigating further into a change of nine, we return again to the fact that all is one transformation. In that one transformation comes form, change—and beginning.

"The pure and light rises and becomes heaven. The gross and heavy sinks to become earth. Pouring force, harmonized into subtle energy, becomes people.

"Thus heaven and earth contain all the essence and all things develop and flourish." (L)

18 | The Duke Who Saw Yin and Yang

Duke Liu (before tenth century BCE) was deeply dedicated. His territory was broad and long. He climbed to the ridge-tops and watched the shifting of yin and yang—the shadow and light on the hillsides—and observed the courses of the streams and springs. Accordingly, he divided his armies into three divisions, measured the marshes and springs, set out the fields for planting, and calculated the times for sunset and dawn. (CP)

19 | Nothing It Doesn't Do

There is life; life births more life. There is form; form leads to more form. There is sound; sound makes more sound. There is color; color becomes more color. There is flavor; flavor yields more flavor.

The life that comes from the birthless may die, yet the life that gives life is endless. Form is in place now, yet the form that gives form is endless. Sound is heard, yet the sound that gives sound is endless. Color is obvious, yet the color that creates color is endless. Flavor has presence, yet the flavor that gives flavor is endless. All this should be recognized with no effort.

All things are combinations of yin and yang, soft and hard, brief and lasting, round and square, alive and dead, hot and cold, floating and sinking, grand and modest, absent and present, mysterious or obvious, sweet and bitter, fetid and fragrant.

It may seem that this world isn't conscious and doesn't have abilities, but there is nothing that isn't within its scope and nothing it doesn't do. (L)

23

20 | How the World Arrives at Order

Neither heaven nor earth can do everything on their own. The sages cannot do anything by themselves. The ten thousand things cannot fully function without each other.

Therefore, heaven's role is to produce life and protect it. Earth's role is to produce forms and support them. The sages' role is to teach change. The role of the ten thousand things is to find what is suitable for each one.

Naturally, heaven has its brevity, earth has its duration, the sages have their difficulties, and the creatures have their lots. Why is that?

That which produces life and protects it cannot produce form or give support. Form and support cannot teach change. Teaching change cannot show the creatures how to find what's suitable. Finding what's suitable cannot go beyond order.

Therefore, this is the way of heaven and earth: all is either yin or yang. The sages teach: all is either benevolence or justice. When the ten thousand things find what's suitable, they will reach what is soft and hard. This is how everything finds what is fitting and yet does not go beyond the proper order. (L)

21 | How the Universe Started

There was a beginning. Before there was a beginning, there was another beginning. Before that beginning was another beginning.

There is something. There is nothing. Before there was something, there was nothing. Before there was nothing, there was nothing before there was the start of nothing. If there was more nothing, would we really know whether something was really the result of nothing?

Now, I cannot really know whether what I've said was worth saying. Could my conclusion be worth nothing? (Z)

22 | All Things and I Are One

Under heaven, nothing is as huge as the tip of an autumn hair or as tiny as a great mountain. Nothing is as long-lived as an infant who dies too soon, or as short-lived as the immortal Peng Zu.

Heaven, earth, and I were born together, and all things, including me, are one. Thus, all things and I are one. Since we are already one, what more needs to be said? (Z)

23 | There Is No Limit to Knowledge

My life has a limit, but knowledge has no limit. Therefore, when the limited is used to pursue the limitless, it is dangerous. If we know this and still pursue knowledge, the danger cannot be avoided.

One should not pursue excellence to the point of fame. One should not seek to control evil to the point of punishment.

Only by following the channels can one preserve one's body throughout one's entire life, nourish one's family, and complete one's years. (Z)

24 | The Wisdom of the Cook

King Wei (r. 369–319 BCE) watched his cook, Pao Ding, cutting up an ox. The man probed with his hand, leaned with his shoulder, planted his foot, and pushed with his knee. A large piece fell open with a tearing sound. The cook's knife kept working with regular, steady slices as if he was moving to the Mulberry Forest rain dance or swaying to the rhythm of ancient Jing Shou music.

"Ahh, how admirable," said King Wei. "How did you get such skill?"

Pao Ding put his knife down and answered: "Your servant most loves Tao, which goes beyond skill.

"When I first began to cut up oxen, I saw nothing but an ox. After three years, I no longer saw the whole ox. I approached it with my spirit rather than my eyes. I did not use conscious thought and instead I let my spirit act freely.

"I sought the natural divisions. My knife slipped along the big seams, found large openings and took full advantage of them. I didn't need to slice through tendons or saw through big bones.

"There are joints and spaces. The edge of the knife has no thickness. When a blade of no thickness enters the seams, see how easily it moves! The blade has more than enough room! Mine is still sharp after nineteen years.

"Every so often, I come to a complicated joint and I see that there may be some difficulty. I proceed carefully, observe thoroughly, and move slowly. Then, by the slightest movement of the knife, the part separates quickly and falls to the ground like a clod of earth.

"Then I stand up, knife in hand, look around unhurriedly, and wipe my knife and sheath it with great satisfaction.

"A good cook changes his knife every year because it has dulled. An ordinary cook changes his knife monthly, especially if he chips the blade. My knife has been in use for nineteen years. I have cut up several thousand oxen, and yet its edge is as sharp as if it had just left the whetstone."

"Excellent!" King Wei exclaimed. "I have heard Pao Ding speak and have learned how to nourish life!" (Z)

25 | The Realized Person

If people sleep in damp places, their backs will hurt and half their bodies will be stiff—but would it be the same case with an eel?

If people were made to live in trees, they would be scared and anxious—but what about monkeys?

And yet, do any of those three—people, eels, or monkeys—know their rightful places in life?

People eat livestock raised on grass and grain. Deer eat grass. Centipedes find small snakes sweet. Owls and crows delight in mice. And yet, do any of these four know what true taste is?

The male ape wants a female. Elk and deer seek mates. Fish chase after other fish. The ladies Mao Qiang and Li Ji (d. 651 BCE) were called the most beautiful of women, but fishes that saw them dove away, birds that glimpsed them swooped off, and elk and deer that saw them ran away. And yet, did any of these four know what true feminine beauty in the world might be?

In my view, the doctrines of benevolence and righteousness and the paths of right and wrong are completely mixed up and confused. How could I know how to sort them out?

Nie Que said: "If you do not know what is beneficial or harmful, then would a Realized Person know what is beneficial or harmful?"

"Realized Persons are spiritual," replied Wang Ni. "Great lakes might boil around them and they would not feel hot. Rivers might freeze and they would not feel cold. Lightning and thunder might cleave mountains and winds might whip the oceans, yet they would not be afraid. Accordingly, they can ride the clouds and the air, mount the sun and the moon, and wander beyond the four seas. Neither death nor life will change them, so why should they bother with the doctrines of benefit or harm?" (Z)

26 | The Sage

Qu Quezi questioned Chang Wuzi: "I heard the master say, 'The sage does not pursue worldly affairs. The sage is unconcerned with advantage, is unafraid of harm, takes no joy in seeking favors, and is not confined by conventional methods. When the sage is silent, something is still said. When the sage speaks, no argument is in it. When traveling, the sage is beyond the dust and dirt of the world.' The master considered this just an endless torrent of words, but I thought that it revealed the endlessly moving Tao. May I ask what you think?"

"Even if the legendary Yellow Emperor (r. 2698–2598 BCE) had heard this, he would have been dazzled," said Chang Wuzi. "How could that venerable master have known enough to understand it? On the other hand, you are in too much of a hurry to reach a conclusion. You see an egg and immediately expect a cock crowing at dawn. You see a pellet and instantly want a roast owl. Let me try to explain loosely, and I hope you'll listen in the same loose way.

"Who can stand beside the sun and the moon and clasp all the universe? Who can merge with everything, leave what is confused and muddled, and be both servant and lord?

"Compared to everyone that toils and bustles, the sage seems stupid and foolish. However, the sage gathers ten thousand years into a single pure moment, knows that everything advances along a natural course, and remembers that all things always blend together." (Z)

27 | Look Up, Look Down

Raise your head and look up at the movements of heaven. Look down and examine the patterns of earth. Then you will know all causes from dark to light.

Trace things to their beginning, follow them through to the end. Then you'll know all that can be said about life and death.

Learn the essence and energy of all things and all the variations of wandering souls, and then you will know the form and the nature of ghosts and spirits alike.

Heaven and earth are always together: follow that and never separate from that.

Know the cycles of all the ten thousand things and that Tao flows through the entire world. Don't go beyond that. Instead, move with it and don't waver. Rejoice in heaven, know its dictates, and never be out of step with it. Be at peace with your place and cherish kindness. Be capable of love.

Never try to exceed the changing patterns of heaven and earth. Don't neglect the turnings and completions of all things. Follow thoroughly the Tao of day and night. Then the spirits will not be troublesome and the changes will not be restricted by form. (YJ)

28 | Life Comes from the Birthless

Master Liezi lived on a small plot of land in the state of Zheng. For forty years, no one recognized him for the sage he was. The prince, ministers, and the officials just saw him as a commoner.

When famine fell upon the state, Liezi wanted to move to the state of Wei. His disciples said: "You are about to go away without any definite time to return. We venture to approach you and hope for some last instructions. Do you have any words from Master Huqiu Zilin to tell us?"

Liezi smiled and said: "Do you suppose that my master said much? However, I will try to repeat what I once overheard him saying to his friend, Ba'hun Maoren.

"There is life and there is the birthless. There is change and the unchanging. The birthless gives birth to life. The unchanging brings about the change that changes.

"Life never fails to produce life. Change never fails to produce change. Hence, the everlasting produces everlasting change. Everlasting life produces everlasting change.

"At no time are we without life. At no time are we without change. That is so of yin and yang. It is so with the four seasons. The birthless cannot be doubted. The unchanging always brings about returning. That returning is limitless and endless without fail. Its Tao is never exhausted."

The *Book of the Yellow Emperor* states: "The Valley Spirit never dies. It is called the Mysterious Feminine. When we open the door to the Mysterious Feminine, we find that it is the root of heaven and earth. It is softer than soft and works without effort."

Thus, all creatures spring from the birthless. All change that creatures experience comes from the changeless.

It births itself and changes itself. It has its own form and color. It knows itself and has its own strength. It can vanish or cease on its own. And yet, to call it "birth" or "change," to say that it has "form and color," to say that it has "knowledge and strength" or that it can "vanish or cease"—all that would be wrong. (L)

29 | The Master Carpenter

Shi, a master carpenter, was traveling when he came to an enormous oak tree at the center of the local marketplace that was used as an altar to the earth. It was so large that several thousand head of cattle could be hidden behind it. Its trunk measured a hundred spans in diameter. It rose up so high that it blocked the view of a mountain, and its crown was so lofty that it was eighty cubits above the ground. At least ten of its branches were thick enough that a boat could have been hollowed out of them. But the carpenter did not even bother to look at the tree and kept walking.

His apprentice was impressed by the tree and ran after him, saying: "Since I've followed you carrying your ax and supplies, I've never seen such beautiful timber as this. But you, sir, won't even stop to look. Why?"

"Stop! Do not speak any more of this! This wood is worthless. A boat made from it would sink. A coffin would promptly rot. Furniture made from it would fall apart. A door would ooze sap. A pillar would become insect-riddled. That is no valuable timber. It is useless. But that is why the tree has lived so long."

During the carpenter's return journey, the tree appeared to him in a dream. "What other tree would you compare me to? Will you compare me to one of your ornamental trees? The hawthorn? The pear? Orange, grapefruit, or any fruit tree?

"As soon as their fruit is ripe, workers pluck their fruit and strip them crudely. They break the large limbs and tear off small branches. The trees are productive, but that makes their lives bitter. They cannot finish their natural lifespans but come to an early end while they are still growing. This vulgar world hurts them—and how true that is of everything else!

"For a long time, I have asked why I am so useless. Now that I'm close to my death, I understand. My uselessness has, in fact, been of the greatest use to me.

"Suppose that I was useful. Would I have reached my great size? Moreover, you and I are both beings. How can one being pass judgment over another? How is it that you, a damn worthless man, should think to judge me as a worthless tree?

Carpenter Shi awoke and thought about the dream and talked to his apprentice.

"If it's so set on being useless," said the apprentice, "why is it here acting as the altar to the earth?"

"Quiet! Say no more! It simply grew here. If we criticize, it shows that we don't really understand. Even if the tree wasn't used as an altar, how likely would it be to get cut down? Furthermore, it has survived in a way that most people would not understand. If you use ordinary assumptions of fair and valuable, you'll be far off the mark." (Z)

30 | The Disabled Man

Shu was disabled. His jowls sagged to hide his navel, his shoulders were higher than his head, his neck bone pointed to the sky, his five organs were pushed upward, and his thigh bones were as spindly as ribs.

He was able to eke out a living by sharpening needles and taking in washing. When he could get jobs winnowing and cleaning rice, he was able to earn enough to feed ten people. When others were drafted to go to war, he went to see them off. When the village was called to contribute men and money to a great public work, no assignments were given to him because of his problems. When assistance was given to the disabled, he received five large measures of grain and ten bundles of firewood.

If such a disabled man was able to support himself and complete his life, how much more lucky he would have been to also be "disabled" in virtue! (Z)

31 | The Usefulness of Being Useless

Confucius (551–479 BCE) was living for a time in the state of Chu. One day, Jie Yu, known as the Madman of Chu, happened to pass the gate and call out:

"Phoenix, oh Phoenix! How your virtue has faded! The future is not to be expected, the past is not to be found again! When Tao prevails in the world, the sage can be of service. When there is no Tao in the world, the sage can only try to survive. At this time, it's all one can do to escape disaster.

"Happiness is as light as a feather, and yet no one knows how to lift it. Disaster is as heavy as the earth, and yet no one knows how to dodge it. Let all this go! Give up trying to teach virtue! You are in danger! Danger! The ground is marked against you. Hurry on!

"I avoid being infatuated! I avoid being entangled! I avoid injury as I make my way. I may stop for a moment or go around, but my feet will not be hurt!"

Mountains are weakened by their own trees. Oil is fried by its own fire. Cinnamon trees are gouged and chopped down. The valuable lacquer tree suffers endless hacks.

Everyone knows the usefulness of being useful. No one knows the usefulness of being useless. (Z)

32 | Covering One's Ears

A man found a great bronze bell that he wanted to carry away on his back, but it was too big. He thought to break it into smaller pieces and so he hit the bell with a mallet. The bell rang mightily.

Afraid that others would hear and try to take the bell from him, the man covered his ears.

That he didn't want others to hear makes sense, but that he should cover his own ears doesn't make sense. Aren't rulers who don't want to hear of their own errors just like that man? (LBW)

33 | The Truthful Ministers

Once, Marquis Wen (d. 396 BCE) held a banquet and ordered his grand officers to offer their opinions of him. Some spoke of their lord's benevolence, some mentioned his moral principles, and others lauded his wisdom.

When it was Ren Zuo's turn, he said: "My lord is an unworthy ruler. When he conquered Zhongshan, he did not reward his younger brother but instead rewarded his son. Thus I know that my lord is unworthy."

The marquis reacted with an angry look and Ren Zuo quickly left.

Then it was Minister Di Huang's turn to speak: "My lord is a worthy ruler. Your subject has heard that when a lord is worthy, his ministers speak truthfully. Just now, Ren Zuo spoke sincerely and so I know that my lord is worthy."

The marquis was pleased and asked, "Should I let him return?"

"Why not? A loyal minister will not flee death. Ren Zuo will still be at the gate."

Di Huang went to the gate and Ren Zuo was indeed there. When he returned, the marquis descended the staircase to welcome him. In time, Zuo was promoted. (LBW)

34 | The Power of an Ugly Man

Duke Ai (r. 494–468 BCE) put this case to Confucius:

"An ugly man named Ai Tai Tuo lived in the state of Wei. When men were around him, they couldn't tear themselves away. When women saw him, they said to their parents: 'I would rather be his concubine than the wife of any other man.' There were ten such cases.

"He never tried to dominate a discussion and always seemed to agree with everyone. Since he did not have the position of an emperor, he couldn't spare others from death. He didn't have any wealth to fill others' bellies. In fact, he was so ugly that he could have terrified anybody in the world. He had to get along without bothering anyone. He didn't know any more than the four sides of his village. Yet men and women sought him out. I wondered what made him different? So I summoned him and observed him.

"Certainly, he was the ugliest man in the world. But he had not been in my court for more than a few months when I began to truly consider him. Before a year had passed, I found that I had confidence in him. Since I did not have a prime minister, I wanted to entrust the affairs of state to him. But my offer made him gloomy, and he clearly wanted to decline. Although I felt awkward, I pressed him to take office anyway. In a little while, though, he left and went away. What kind of man was he?"

"I was once on a mission to the state of Qi," replied Confucius. "I saw piglets trying to suckle at their dead mother.

But they became confused after a while and they ran off. The mother pig could no longer see them; she was not the same as she was before. What the piglets loved about their mother was not her body, but what animated her body. Similarly, when a man dies in battle and is buried, he has no use for medals and plumes, just as a man who has lost his feet has no use for shoes. In both those cases, there is no reason to love any of those things because the need for them is gone.

"When women become royal consorts, they do not clip their fingernails or pierce their ears. When a man is newly married, he doesn't go anywhere and he takes time off from his duties. If such concern can be taken for the body, we should show the same concern for people's virtue! Now, Ai Tai Tuo was trusted before he even said a word. He made no effort and yet people loved him. Rulers wanted to give their states to him, worrying only that he might refuse. This was because his powers were complete and his virtue took no form."

"What do you mean when you say that his powers were complete?"

"Death and life, survival and destruction, failure and success, poverty and wealth, worthiness and worthlessness, slander and fame, starvation and thirst, cold and hot—these are all matters of circumstance and the movement of life.

"Right in front of us, day follows night but none of our knowledge can tell us the reasons why. But that must not disturb your harmony. It must not wreck the treasure house of your spirit. If you can balance and accept this all and never let

43

your joy be disrupted; if you are never disturbed day or night, so that it seems like everything is like spring; if you can blend with all of life and with the seasons in your mind—then your powers will be complete." (Z)

35 | What the Wise See

Take one part yin and one part yang and call that Tao: that maintains goodness and completes the natures of all things.

The benevolent call that the essence of benevolence. The wise call that true wisdom. The common people use this every day without being conscious of it. What few people see, the cultivated person knows.

It is in every kindness. It can be stored up and used. It drives the ten thousand things without any need for sagely participation. From the start, it's abundantly virtuous and it is the greatest activity.

Great activity leads to wealth, and abundant virtue leads to new days. Life upon life leads to ongoing change.

Heaven completes all that we see, earth manifests all inherent principles. By exhaustively counting everything, we gain foresight, and we can conduct all matters throughout all their different stages. What is called divine is only a matter of inestimable yin and yang. (YJ)

36 | Forgetting Ugliness for Virtue

A lame hunchback with no lips was the counselor to Duke Ling (c. 534–492 BC). Duke Ling was so pleased with the advice that he came to see other men as having overly long and skinny necks.

Another man with a goiter as large as an earthenware jar advised Duke Huan (r. 685–643 BCE). Duke Huan was so pleased that he also saw other men as having overly long and skinny necks.

Thus, if one's virtue is extraordinary, one's appearance will be overlooked.

When people do not forget what should-be-forgotten, and forget what-should-not-be-forgotten, that's called true oblivion.

The ancient sages kept roaming. Knowledge was treacherous, promises were glue, morality was knotty, and labor was commerce.

The sages never schemed, so why would they injure themselves with knowledge? They did no chopping, so why would they need glue? They had no loss, so why would they need knots? They had nothing to sell, so why would they need commerce?

Instead of these four problems they had heaven's nourishment. With such nourishment, they had the food of heaven. Since they had the food of heaven, what need did they have to exploit other people?

They looked like people, but they did not have the passions of people. They looked like other people and lived among them, but they did not have other people's desires. They were not hurt by the problems of what was and wasn't.

How few the number of such sages, and yet how grand and great they were—and how singularly complete they were in heaven. (Z)

37 | The Philosophy of Hui Shi

Hui Shi (380–305 BCE) had so many techniques that his writings filled five carts, but his Tao was mistaken and contradictory and his words were far off the mark. Taking one thing after another, he would say:

> That which is of the greatest largeness has no outside and may be called the great one. That which is so small it has no inside may be called the small one.

> That which has no thickness cannot be built up yet it is a thousand kilometers in size.

> Heaven is as low as earth and the mountain may be as level as the marsh.

> The sun at noon is setting. What is born is dying.

> What is greatly alike is different from what is slightly alike. These are called little similarities and differences. The ten thousand things are completely alike and completely different. These are called the great similarities of great differences.

> The south is unlimited and yet is limited.

> I went to Yue today, but I arrived yesterday.

> Joined hoops cannot be separated.

> I know where the center of the world is: it is north of Yan and south of Yue.

> If the ten thousand things are flooded with love, then heaven and hearth are of one body.

Thus Hui Shi was known by everyone in the world and was considered an eloquent debater. Other debaters eagerly tried to follow him, using such arguments as:

An egg has feathers. A chicken has three feet. The state of Ying encompasses the whole world. A dog can be called a sheep. Horses have eggs. A tadpole has a tail. Fire is not hot. A mountain puts forth a voice. A wheel does not roll on the ground. An eye does not see. A finger cannot touch. Where you come to may not be the end. A turtle is longer than a snake. The carpenter's square is not square. A compass cannot be round. A chisel does not have a handle. The shadow of a flying bird does not move. As swift as an arrow head may be, there are times when it is neither moving nor at rest. A dog is not a hound. A bay horse and a black bull added together make three. A white dog is black. A motherless colt never had a mother. If from a stick ten centimeters long you take half off every day, in a myriad ages it will never be shortened.

Thus the debaters contended endlessly with Hui Shi. Huan Tuan and Gongsun Long were among these debaters. They tried to trick others and change their ideas. They were fierce in argument, but they never changed anyone's minds and instead boxed them in. Hui Shi used his knowledge to make novel arguments. That was the very basis of his approach. (Z)

38 | Can People Be Without Desire?

"Can people be without desire?" Hui Shi asked Zhuangzi.

"They can."

"But if people are without desire, can we still call them human?"

"Tao gives them their appearance. Heaven gives them their form. Why couldn't we call them human?"

"So if you call them human, can they be without desire?"

Zhuangzi said: "You don't understand what I mean by desire. What I call 'without desire' means people do not let 'good' and 'bad' bring them harm. They remain natural and do not try to add to life."

"If they didn't try to add to life, then how would they have bodies?"

"Tao gives them appearance. Heaven gives them form. They do not let 'good' and 'bad' bring them harm. Now you, sir, deal with the spirit as if it's something outside of yourself. You waste your vital essence in effort. You recite your theories as you lean against a tree, and doze off embracing the withered trunk of a parasol tree. Heaven chose you and gave you form, but you only babble about what's 'solid' and 'white.'" (Z)

39 | Roaming Free and Easy

Hui Shi said to Zhuangzi: "I have a big tree that people call the stink tree. It has a huge swollen trunk that is too gnarled for a measuring line. Its small branches are so twisted that neither a compass nor a square can be applied to them. The trees are planted by the roadside, but no artisan will even look at them. Now, your words, sir, seem great, but are useless. Anyone would spurn them."

"Have you never seen a wildcat or a weasel?" Zhuangzi replied. "It crouches down and hides waiting for something to come along, then leaps east and west, high and low, until it is caught in a trap or dies in a net. Then there is the yak, large enough to be a cloud hanging in the sky. It is big—but it cannot catch mice. You, sir, have a large tree that you worry is useless. Why don't you plant it in a village that has nothing else, or grow it in the unspoiled and open wilderness? Then you might ramble idly beside it, roaming free and easy, and sleep beneath it. No ax would chop it and nothing would hurt it. What uselessness is there to distress you?" (Z)

40 | White Dog, Black Dog

Yang Zhu's younger brother, Bu, went out one day dressed all in white.

Rain fell and soaked him, so he came home and changed into black clothes. When he came out of his room, his dog did not recognize him and ran at him barking. This made Bu angry, and he was about to beat the dog when Yang Zhu stopped him.

"Don't hit him. You are no smarter than him! Suppose that one day your dog went away white and came home black. Wouldn't you find that strange?" (L)

41 | The True Person

If you know how heaven acts, then you also fully know how people should act.

If you know how heaven acts and how heaven makes life, then you also know how people should act.

You may know what you know, but cultivate learning what you do not yet know.

Live your life fully. Don't get cut off in youth or in midlife. This is all the wisdom you need.

But even so, there is a problem. Knowledge needs confirmation, and until then nothing is clearly settled. How do I know that what I call heaven is not also human, and that what I call human is not also heaven?

That's why we need a True Person—to attest to true knowledge. (Z)

42 | The True Person of the Past

Who can be called a True Person?

The True Person of ancient times did not reject the few, did not aggressively pursue success, and did not scheme to achieve a career.

In this way, even if they committed some excess, they needed no remorse. If they had some success, they did not covet things for themselves.

Therefore, they could climb heights without fear, dive into water and not get wet, plunge into fire and not be burned. It was because of their wisdom that they could rise above the false and enter Tao as they did. (Z)

43 | Serving Others

The True Person of ancient times was not giddy over life and was unafraid of death. They entered life without delight and they left without protest. They went briskly, they came briskly and that was all.

They did not forget their beginning, and they did not complain about their ending. If they received something, they were thankful, and if they missed something, they just went back to their path. That's called "not giving up Tao in your heart and not trying to push heaven."

Therefore, their hearts were steady, their looks were calm, and their foreheads were unlined. For them, bitter cold was as mild as autumn, hot weather was like spring, and their emotions passed from one to the other like the turning of the four seasons. They felt that all things had a place—and yet they didn't think of that as limited.

In the past, even if the sages went to war, they would rather have lost a nation than have lost the hearts of the people. They brought benefit and brilliance to everything and all creatures without preferential love for anyone.

Hence, one who delights in goodness is not a sage. One who favors oneself is not benevolent. One who calculates heavenly opportunity is unworthy. One who withholds gain and loss is no cultivated person. One concerned with action and fame is lost and is no scholar. One who forgets oneself is not true and cannot serve others.

Those like Hu Bujie, Wu Guang (d. 208 BCE), Boyi and Shuqi (eleventh century BCE), Ji Zi, Ji Ta, and Shenfu Di all served others and fulfilled what others wanted fulfilled. They did not seek to fulfill what they themselves might have wanted. (Z)

44 | Breathing to the Heels

The True Person of ancient times slept without dreaming and awoke without care. Their food was plain.

Their breathing was deep. The True Person breathed to their heels. Most people breathe to their throats. Bent and tight, they quarrel and vomit words. Their desires are old and deep, but they are shallow when it comes to knowing the opportunities of heaven. (Z)

45 | The Disciples Outwit Their Master

There was once an old sage named Wang Shen who loved to retreat to a cool cave to read. He had many disciples. When the time came for their lessons one day, a student went to the mouth of the cave to say: "Master, it is time for our lessons."

A mischievous thought came to the master: "Let's see if you can talk me into leaving this cave."

The disciples tried many appeals and ruses, but the old man laughed off each attempt. At last, one of the pupils said:

"Oh master, we admit that we cannot get you out of the cave. But if you were to come out here, we could surely get you back in!"

The old man immediately came out and defied them to force him back into the cave. It was only then that he realized that his students had tricked him. (FT)

46 | I Heard of Tao

Nanbo Zikui asked Nu Yu: "You are old, but your complexion is like a child's. Why is that?"

"I heard of Tao."

"Is it possible to learn of Tao?"

"Hush! Do you think you could?" Nu Yu said. "Mr. Buliang Yi had the potential of a sage, but he did not have the Tao of a sage. I had the Tao of a sage, but I didn't have the potential of a sage.

"I wanted to teach him and make him into a sage. It wasn't easy for someone with a sage's Tao to teach someone with a sage's talent. I tried to foster him and talk to him.

"After three days, he was able to transcend the world. I continued. After seven days, he was able to transcend thoughts of material things. With that settled, I continued. After nine days, he was able to transcend life itself. Having accomplished that, he was as clear as the morning. With that, he could see his aloneness. Once he could do that, he transcended past and present. After that, he entered into a state beyond birth or death. Having entered that, he knew the life of life-without-birth.

"This is the substance of what he attained: everything was sent, everything was received, everything was destroyed, everything was completed. That's called peace within strife.

"'Peace in strife' means the completion that comes after strife." (Z)

47 | Afraid of the World's Collapse

A man who lived in the state of Qi was scared that heaven and earth would collapse and fall apart, which would have left him without a place to live, and so he could neither sleep nor eat.

Xiao Zhi, seeing his distress, tried to explain: "Heaven is filled with energy: energy is everywhere. Think of how you inhale and exhale—the same process is going on in heaven. Why worry that heaven will collapse and fall apart?"

"Heaven may be filled with energy. But what about the sun, moon, and stars? Won't they fall on us?"

"The sun, moon, and stars are part of a massive energy, and they are just twinkling lights. Even if they were to fall, they would not harm us."

"Then what if the earth were to fall apart?"

"The earth is a great combination of matter, filling and blocking up the four corners of space. Matter is everywhere. Besides, the ground is walked upon all day long. It is treaded and stamped and in the end the sun will still move above the earth. Again, how can you be afraid that anything will be lost?"

The man was reassured, and Xiao Zhi was also glad.

But Chang Luzi heard them and laughed: "Rainbows and reflections, clouds and mist, wind and rain, the four seasons—these result from heaven's boundless energy. Mountains and hills, rivers and seas, metal and rock, fire and wood—these result from the earth's boundless formations.

"You know the fullness of energy. You know the fullness of matter. How can you say that they will never be destroyed? This world is but a tiny speck in vast space. We are in the middle of an enormity that is bigger than big. It is hard to see the ends, hard to reduce things enough to understand which things are solid, or to measure and understand anything. You are worrying about what is quite far off. Why keep talking about things falling apart? It's a problem that doesn't even exist yet.

"Besides, heaven and earth will not collapse as long as they continue to be together. While that remains so, they cannot be destroyed. Until the time for destruction comes, why be afraid?"

Hearing all this, Liezi also laughed: "To talk of heaven and earth being destroyed is unnecessary. Whether the world will be destroyed or not, I certainly don't know. If it happens, it will be the same for everyone alike. Just as the living don't know anything of the dead, and the dead know nothing of the living, it's futile for you to keep talking back and forth. Whether the world should fall apart or not—why should we worry ourselves over it?" (L)

48 | Hide the World in the World

A big piece of ground supports me. I labor on it all my life. I should enjoy it when I grow old and find rest in it when I die. Whatever is good for my life will be good for my death too.

If you hide a boat beyond a marsh and deep in a ravine, you may think that your boat is safe, but strong people might still carry it off in the middle of the night without you ever knowing it. You can try to hide anything, large or small, in any place you deem suitable, but it can still disappear.

Instead, if you hide the world in the world, then it would be impossible for anything to vanish. That would be the bigger aspect of reality. (Z)

49 | I'm Improving

Yan Hui (521?–481 BCE), said to his teacher, Confucius, "I'm improving."

"How so?"

"I've let go of benevolence and righteousness."

"Acceptable. But not enough."

On another day, Hui saw Confucius, and said again: "I'm improving."

"How so?"

"I've let go of conduct and music."

"Acceptable. But still not enough."

On yet another day, Hui saw Confucius and said: "I'm improving."

"How so?"

"I sit and let go."

Confucius straightened up. "How do you let go?"

"I relax my limbs and body, turn away from perception and understanding, leave my body, and put thought aside. I merge with the greatness that runs through everything. That's what I call to sit and let go."

Confucius said, "How good when merging is the same as emptiness. If you can transform yourself into nothingness and be constant in it, then that's a worthwhile outcome indeed! If you can do that, I would ask to learn from you!" (Z)

50 | Learning Takes Perseverance

Liezi and his friend, Bai Gaozi, studied for a long time with Master Lao Shang. After Liezi had progressed far enough in learning Tao, he rode the wind back home.

Yin Sheng heard of Liezi's return and he asked to become a disciple. Liezi accepted him and Yin moved into his new teacher's home as was the custom. A few months passed, but after receiving no apparent lessons, Yin begged to learn the secret art of Tao.

He asked ten times, but each time Liezi did not reply. Upset, Yin finally threatened to leave, but still Liezi gave him no answer. So Yin left.

However, he could not stop thinking about the situation for months afterward. Consequently, he went back and asked to become a disciple again. Liezi said: "Why are you coming and going again?"

"I asked for instruction before," replied Yin, "But you would not teach me and I was unhappy. Now I'm not so sure what happened and so I came back."

"I once thought that you were smart. How did you fall so low? Listen, and I will tell you what I learned from my own teacher.

"Gaozi and I lived with our master, and yet for three years, my heart did not dare to distinguish between right and wrong. My lips did not dare to speak of good or harm. Eventually, my master began to glance at me.

"After five years, my heart could consider right and wrong, and my lips could speak of good and harm. Then my master's face relaxed and he smiled.

"After seven years, I followed the thoughts of my heart, and did not concern myself with right and wrong. I followed the speech of my lips, but did not need to talk of good or harm. Then my master began to gesture for me to sit on the mat beside him.

"After nine years, my heart had the right inclination. My lips stayed closed. I did not know of right or wrong, good or harm whether for myself or for others. I did not know my master as my teacher, nor did I know my friend Gaozi as my companion. Internal and external combined. There was no difference between eye and ear, ear and nose, nose and mouth. All were the same. My heart stilled, my body dissolved, my bones and flesh fused. I did not know where I was or where I was going. The wind blew me from east to west as if I was dry chaff or fallen leaves. Did the wind ride me? Or did I ride the wind?

"Now, you have not even passed a rainy season inside my house and you have already shown your unhappiness three times. You can barely stand, let alone channel energy through your flake of a body. You can barely get across the dirt, even for a bit. So how can you expect to walk in the void or ride the wind?"

Abashed, Yin Sheng was struck dumb and did not dare reply. (L)

51 | Remembering What Made You

Han Xin (d. 196 BCE) was a great general. His family was poor and his father died when Han was still a child. Others in his neighborhood looked down on him and he frequently had to beg for his meals. However, he had a keen interest in military strategy and he loved to practice the sword.

Once, when he was suffering from hunger, an old woman gave him some food. He promised to repay her one day, but she didn't take him seriously. At another time, a bully saw Han carrying a sword and challenged him to either fight him or humiliate himself by crawling between the bully's legs. Han realized that he would become a criminal if he killed the man so he crawled between the bully's legs. All the townspeople jeered him.

After becoming a famous general and statesman years later, Han Xin returned to his hometown and found the old woman who had fed him. He gave her 1,750 ounces of gold. He also found the bully, and instead of taking revenge, he made the man a lieutenant in his army. Han said: "This man is a hero. I could have killed him when he humiliated me— but then I would not have become famous. I endured humiliation so I could preserve myself for greater accomplishments in the future." (FT)

52 | The House of Peace

There was once a retired official named Zhang who was the patriarch of an enormous family estate with one thousand members and nine generations living together. There was utter harmony in the family, and it was said that there was never a single argument among them. The men never competed with one another, the women were never jealous of each other, the children never bickered or snatched each other's toys, and even the dogs never took another one's bones. It was truly a house of peace.

News of this reached the emperor and he went to see for himself. He paid a surprise visit and the family was both astonished and greatly honored to receive their ruler.

"Honored elder," said the emperor, "what is the secret to the peace in your home?"

Now, Patriarch Zhang was elderly and weak and he was overcome to be in the presence of the emperor himself. He motioned for his great grandchildren to help him write out a response to the emperor. They prepared his ink, brush, and paper, after which the old man wrote a single word in beautiful calligraphy.

At first, as the word began to appear, they saw the word for a "knife's edge" and everyone was startled. Then the old man added the word "heart" below that, and then everyone knew what he had written: forbear. (FT)

53 | People Flourish in Tao

Fish flourish in water. People flourish in Tao.

By flourishing in Tao, there are no troubles and life is assured.

And yet: "Fish don't know that they live in rivers and lakes, people don't know the art of Tao." (Z)

54 | Lamenting Dire Need

Ziyu and Zisang were friends. When it rained constantly for ten days, Ziyu thought, "Zisang might be sick or in trouble." So he wrapped some food and brought it to his friend to eat.

As he approached Zisang's door, he heard a sobbing song, the sounds of a qin (a seven-stringed zither), and the lyrics: "Oh father, oh mother! Oh heaven, oh anyone!" The voice quavered and the words were urgent.

Ziyu went in and asked, "Why are you singing this?"

"I was wondering what caused me to reach such extreme adversity," Zisang replied. "Did my parents want me to be poor? Heaven covers us all impartially, earth supports us all equitably—how could heaven and earth seemingly single me out for scarcity? I've asked repeatedly what might have kept me from succeeding, and yet here I am, in dire misery! It must be my fate!" (Z)

55 | The Way of the Thief

A poor man named Mr. Xiang went to a rich man named Mr. Guo to ask the secret of wealth. Mr. Guo replied: "I am an excellent thief. In my first year, I got just enough. By the second year, I had plenty. By the third year, I reaped a great harvest. Eventually, I found myself the owner of whole villages and districts."

Mr. Xiang was thrilled. That night, he climbed over walls and broke into houses, grabbing everything he could carry. But he was caught after a few days, and by the time the magistrate had fined him and confiscated his meager possessions, he was worse off than before. After he was released, he went back to the rich man and bitterly accused him of lying.

Mr. Guo was taken aback and asked, "How did you set about being a thief?" When the poor man told him, the rich man sighed. "You went about this all wrong! What I steal are the riches of nature. Heaven and earth offer great and plentiful treasures throughout all the seasons. Just look: The fertilizing rain brings ample growth; all I do is I plant my grain and my crops ripen. I build walls and raise buildings with the timber, dirt, and stone of the earth. The forests give me plenty of birds and game and the rivers teem with fish and turtles for me to catch. I steal everything—for everything is given by nature and there is no reprisal for taking anything. But gold, jade, and silk are owned by people, so it's no surprise that you got into trouble!"

Confused, and afraid of being wrong again, Mr. Xiang went to a scholar named Dong Guo.

The scholar said: "Aren't you already a thief by having a body? You steal the blending of yin and yang to live. You inhale air and drink water. Heaven and earth together comprise nature—so how could you claim anything in nature as your possession? To do so is to be truly muddled.

"The rich man's thefts are correct, whereas yours were selfish and brought you trouble.

"No one can avoid having a body, and no one can avoid absorbing parts of the world nor can they be rid of them no matter how much they try. The great principle is to understand the difference between public and private property. If you truly understand this then, which one of us is a thief and which of us is not a thief?" (L)

56 | Nonaction

Nonaction—not false fame.

Nonaction—not strategy and government.

Nonaction—not knowledge and power.

Completely embody the inexhaustible. Roam without a trace. Take what heaven gives and be invisible. Be empty and leave it at that.

When a Realized Person has a heart like a mirror, nothing needs to be done and nothing needs to be gained. Just respond but don't covet, and you can overcome all things without harm. (Z)

57 | Seagulls

A man who lived by the ocean loved seagulls. When he swam each morning, hundreds of gulls splashed around him.

One day his father said, "I've heard that you swim with seagulls each day. I want you to catch a couple of them for me to keep as pets." The man agreed. But when he went down to the sea the next day, the gulls circled in the air and would not come near him.

Thus it is said: "The best speech is to be rid of speech. The best act is no act. Such knowledge is complete wisdom. Anything else is shallow." (L)

58 | The Yellow Emperor Finds the Tao

The Yellow Emperor (r. 2698–2598 BCE) had been on the throne for fifteen years, and everyone in the empire followed him as their ruler.

At first, he maintained a luxurious life, enjoying all the pleasures that his ears and eyes could take in and reveling in every thrill of smell and taste. Eventually, though, he grew depressed. His complexion turned sallow and he felt dull and confused.

This went on for fifteen years. Concerned about the disorder in his empire, the emperor threw all his ingenuity, wisdom, and strength into ruling. And still, he grew more haggard and pale, and he felt even more addled and dim.

At last, the Yellow Emperor sighed deeply and said: "I must have indulged myself so much that it caused these problems. I emphasized myself too much and over-administered the empire. That must be why I have suffered."

Accordingly, he put aside his many plans, left his rich bedroom and his ancestral palace, dismissed his attendants, took off all his dangling bells, reduced the delicacies of his meals, and retired to live in private apartments by the side of the court. There, he calmed his heart and brought his body under control. For three months he did not participate in government affairs.

Toward the end of this time, he fell asleep during the day and he dreamed that he made a journey to the kingdom of Everything-Splendid, situated at an untold distance west of his empire. It was beyond the reach of any ship, vehicle, or trek by foot—a place that only spirits could reach.

This kingdom had no ruler; it simply functioned by itself. Its people had neither desires nor cravings and they lived naturally. They were not obsessed by life nor afraid of death, yet no one died prematurely. They did not have a concept of clans, they were not careless about things, and they were not excessive in love or hate. They did not rebel or resist, but neither were they overly submissive. They did not know about profit or loss. They were as aloof from love and sympathy as they were from worry and fear.

Water could not drown them. Fire could not burn them. If they were cut or flogged, they would show no injuries. If they were touched or prodded, they did not jump. They would just as soon have left their chariots and walked.

They were not particular about the rooms in which they slept. Clouds and mist did not block their vision. Thunder did not disturb their hearing. Physical beauty did not move their hearts. Mountains and valleys were no obstacles to their journeys on foot. They moved like gods.

The Yellow Emperor awoke, glad to have had this dream. He summoned his three highest ministers of state and said: "For three months, I have been living a life of retreat, calming my heart, dressing plainly, and searching for the way of nourishing life and regulating the lives of others. But I could not find the secret. Worn out, I fell asleep and had a dream. Now I know that Tao is not to be sought impetuously. I know this! I understand this! But I can't articulate it fully."

For twenty-eight years after this, the empire was in order, almost as if it was the kingdom of Everything-Splendid. When the emperor died, the people mourned him without stop for two hundred years. (L)

59 | The Island of the Immortals

Liegu'she Mountain was an island of immortals in the distant ocean. The inhabitants nourished themselves on air and dew and abstained from the five grains. Their hearts were as deep and flowing as springs, their demeanors were like dignified women, and they were neither wanton nor lustful. They were foremost among the immortal sages and they knew neither worry nor anger. Sincere and honest in their interactions, always impartial and fair, they would deny themselves before they would deny another. They did not scheme, held nothing back, and never did wrong.

When yin and yang are in constant interchange, the sun and moon are ever bright; the four seasons follow each other; the wind and rain constantly sweep in to benefit everyone; words are always available for learning; every year's crop is constantly abundant; and the soil is always rich.

Then people do not die, all creatures are perfect, and the ghosts make no supernatural wailings. (L)

60 | The First Emperor

When the First Emperor (259–201 BCE) took the throne, the alchemists told him of Penglai, the island of the immortals. Since the emperor was keen to find the elixir of immortality and live forever, he sent several thousand boys and girls out to sea in search of immortals.

Decades later, and after considerable effort and expense, the alchemists had still not found the secret of immortality. They did not want to be punished so they made this excuse: "The herbs of immortality grow on Penglai, but we are thwarted by monstrous whales that keep us from reaching the island. We request a company of archers so that we can shoot the whales when we next see them."

That night, the emperor dreamed that he fought with a sea god. He consulted his scholar, who said: "Sea gods are invisible but they take the form of giant fish, sea serpents, and dragons. Although your majesty has taken care to offer prayers and sacrifices, an evil spirit has appeared. It must be driven away if good spirits are to take its place."

The First Emperor ordered his sailors to prepare the equipment to catch a great fish, and he traveled in person to the coast. He waited with a crossbow to shoot the sea monster himself.

He traveled northward, but found nothing. He did see a great fish and shot and killed it. Then he traveled westward.

He died on the journey, far from the capital. (RH)

61 | Death and Life

Death and life are a matter of fate, just as we always have night and day. It's up to heaven. People have no control over that. That is just the way things are.

Some regard heaven as if it's their father. They try to embody their love for it as their most profound position.

Others hold the emperor in higher esteem than themselves and they are willing to die for him. If only they had the same regard for the truth!

When the springs dry up, fish are stranded together on the ground. They pant on one another and try to moisten each other with spit, but it would be better if they hadn't gotten into such trouble and could have swum freely in the rivers and lakes.

Similarly, when people praise Yao and condemn Jie, it would be better to forget them both and remember the transformations of Tao. (Z)

62 | Peach Blossom Spring

During the reign of Emperor Xiaowu of Jin (362–396), there lived a fisherman named Wuling. One day he sailed upstream, lost track of how far he had gone, and came to a place upon a forest of blooming peach trees several hundred paces deep on both banks of the stream. Fragrant grasses scented the air and petals whirled around him.

The fisherman was enchanted by the sight and kept sailing. When he reached the end of the forest, he found the spring that fed the stream and saw a hill beyond it. Light glinted through a hole in the hillside. The fisherman tied up his boat and went to investigate. At first, the opening was barely large enough for him to crawl through, but it soon opened onto a larger passage and he was able to stand upright. Within twenty or thirty paces, the tunnel opened onto a beautiful valley.

The land was broad and flat, with houses here and there among verdant fields and with mulberry and bamboo surrounding lovely ponds. Paths ran north, south, east, and west across the fields, and he heard crowing roosters and barking dogs from the different farms. Men and women passed back and forth on their daily errands or worked in the fields. From white-haired elder to running child, everyone seemed contented and happy.

The people were startled to see the fisherman and asked where he had come from. One of the crowd invited him into his home, where they set out wine and killed a chicken to feast with him. Others in the village came to greet him. They told him that their forbears had fled trouble during the reign of the First Emperor and to settle in this faraway place. They never went outside their valley after that and had become isolated from the outer world. They asked him what dynasty it was and who was on the throne. The fisherman did his best to answer their questions, but each statement only made the people nod and murmur in wonder.

For several days, he was the guest in the home of one family after another, sharing their good food and wine. In time, though, he had to take his leave. As they parted with him, the people said, "We trust you won't reveal our secret to anyone."

The fisherman crawled out of the tunnel and found his boat, still tied where he had left it. He sailed home and promptly told the governor about all that had happened. The governor sent troops with the fisherman to find the place again, but the more they looked, the more confused the fisherman became. He could not find the way again. (TYM)

81

63 | Rest

Zigong (520–456 BCE), a disciple of Confucius, grew tired of his lessons, and said to his teacher: "I wish I could rest from all this studying."

"There is no rest in life," Confucius replied.

"Never?"

"Someday. Look at the tombs in the wilds, the graves, the burial mounds, the funerary urns: that is rest."

"So death overcomes all! Noble people come to rest just the same as common people are laid down."

"Yes. Now you know. All people want the joys of life but not its bitterness. They think of old age as weariness, but they don't know its pleasures. They regard death as awful, but they don't know that death is rest." (L)

64 | The Four Friends

Four men—Zisi, Ziyu, Zili, and Zilai—met in conversation. One of them said: "Who could have a head of nonaction, life itself as a spine, and death as a rump? Who could know that life and death, existence and demise are all one body? We would like to be friends with such a person!" The four of them looked at each other and burst out laughing. Since their hearts were in such agreement, they became friends.

Soon, Ziyu fell ill and Zisi went to visit.

"How profound is the Maker," said Ziyu, "that I should be twisted the way I am. My back is as crooked as a hunchback, my five organs are squeezed upward in my body, my chin is doubled over my navel, my shoulders are higher than my head, and my neckbone points at the sky." The yin and yang of his energy were out of harmony, yet his heart was peaceful and quiet.

He limped to a well, saw his reflection, and sighed: "Alas, that the Maker should bend me into the shape I am!"

"Do you resent it?" Zizi asked.

"No, why should I resent it? If this goes on, my left arm might change into a rooster. In that case, I could track the phases of the night. Or maybe my right arm will change into a pellet and I could shoot down an owl for roasting. Or maybe my rump will become wheels and my spirit could turn into a horse that I could mount and ride—I'd never need a carriage again!

"When our time comes to leave, we must go along with it. We must take heed peacefully and settle into acceptance without being either too sad or glad. The ancients called this 'loosening the bounds.'

"But one cannot loosen the bounds by oneself—everything is tied up tightly and that is meant to be. Nobody can overcome heaven. That has been long known. So why should I resent this?"

Before long, another one of the four friends, Zilai, also fell ill, panting and gasping as he lay dying. He was surrounded by his weeping wife and children. Zili went to visit and told them: "Hush! Step back! Do not interfere with the transformation!"

"How profound is the Maker," Zili said to Zilai. "What will you become? Where will you go?" Will you become the liver of a mouse? Will you become the arm of an insect?"

"Wherever parents send their child," replied Zilai, "whether it may be east, west, south, or north, the child must follow their orders. One's mother and father are the two wings that keep one vital—perhaps even more so than yin and yang go into making us human. If I am close to my death but do not listen to what I'm told, then I am being disobedient and should be scolded.

"A big piece of ground supports me. I labor on it all my life. I should enjoy it when I grow old and find rest in it when I die. Whatever is good for my life will be good for my death too. Now, there's a great foundry here where metal is being smelted. If the metal were to leap up and say, 'I insist that you forge me into a great sword like the one called Moye,' the smelter would regard that metal as cursed. Likewise, if while I am being refashioned, I were to demand, 'I must be a person, I must be a person!' the smelter would regard me as cursed.

"Heaven and earth are the great foundry and the Maker is the great smelter. How could anything bad happen to us? At the end of our lives, we go to sleep—and sprout again as if awakening." (Z)

65 | The Four Stages of a Person's Life

Between a person's birth and death are four great stages of change: infancy, youth, old age, and death.

In infancy, one's energy is intact, one's will is whole, and one's internal harmony is at its peak. Outside matters are of no concern, and one's virtue needs nothing else.

In youth, one's energy is like an overwhelming cyclone. Desires and concerns overflow. Outside matters are bothersome and one's virtue is scattered.

In old age, one's desires and concerns soften. One values propriety, care, and leisure. Outside matters lose their previous urgency. Although one no longer has the perfection of infancy, neither does one have the problems of youth.

In death, one finally comes to rest, and one returns to the Ultimate. (L)

66 | How the Ancients Viewed Death

Yanzi said: "How perfect was the ancients' view of death! The good come to rest and all are buried. Death is the virtuous border.

"The ancients referred to the dead as homecomers. If the dead are those who have returned home, then the living are those who are still on a journey. No matter how far travelers wander from home, they don't say that they've lost where they live. After all, who wants to be permanently separated from their home and fall into trouble forever?

"But everyone acts as if they have forgotten their homes. No one sees this mistake. Imagine a case where a person leaves their native soil, says goodbye to their relatives, abandons their family and rightful living, and wanders off to the four corners of the earth to never come back. What kind of person would we call that? We'd call such a person crazy.

"Now, imagine another case where another person builds the highest merit of a lifetime; is discerning, clever, and capable; has great fame and reputation; and is celebrated throughout the world. If they never went home either, would we say that they were any better than the first case? Although the world certainly celebrates a smart and clever person, both kinds of people still make the same mistake.

"The world continues to follow one path and not the other. It takes a sage to know what to truly follow and where to truly go." (L)

67 | Self-Possessed

While he was practicing archery with a friend named Ba'hun Wuren, Liezi placed a cup of water on his elbow, drew a bow to its limit, and shot an arrow into the center of a distant target. He immediately shot twice more, one arrow swiftly following the other as if on a line, and they both struck touching the first one. Liezi lowered his bow with a smug look.

Ba'hun Wuren said: "You shot well. But this is not true archery. Suppose you were to climb a high mountain and stand at the edge of a cliff. Could you still shoot well?"

So the two of them climbed a high mountain. At the summit, Ba'hun Wuren walked to the edge of an abyss hundreds of fathoms deep, turned his back, and put half of his foot over the edge. He motioned to Liezi to join him, but Liezi collapsed on the ground drenched in sweat.

Ba'hun Wuren said: "Great archers can shoot whether they are faced with the blinding blue sky above, yawning hell below, or attackers on every side. Their spirit and energy will not change. But you are frightened of what your good eyes show you! How will you ever hit a bull's-eye if you're in real danger?" (L)

68 | The Power of Complete Belief

Fan Zihua was born to great wealth and became famous throughout the nation. He was highly favored by the king and he sat to the right of the three high ministers of state, even though he had no official title. Whoever his shrewd eyes favored was promoted. Whoever he slandered was dismissed or banished. Fawners thronged his hall every morning.

Zihua encouraged these hangers-on to compete with one another. He had no qualms if clever people bullied the dim-witted or the strong crushed the weak. He amused himself with this drama day and night, even if others whispered that it was the most vulgar display in the land.

One day, two of his leading disciples, He Sheng and Ziba, went on a journey. After traveling through the wilds, they put up for the night in the hut of an old peasant named Shang Qiukai. During that night's conversation, the two chortled over Zihua's prestige and influence, how he had the power of life and death, and how he could decide between wealth and ruin.

Qiukai lived meagerly; he was always hungry and cold and in search for any little chance of a better life. He crept beneath the window to eavesdrop. After having heard about Fan Zihua, he gathered a few provisions in a basket and set off the next day for Zihua's gate.

Zihua's followers were a worldly lot. They wore rich silk and rode in high carriages. They strolled with imperious airs. They saw that Qiukai was old and weak, and that he had a

sunburned face, dim eyes, ragged clothes, and a tattered cap. They thought little of him and so they mocked him, lied to him, blocked his way, punched him, tripped him, and pushed him around as they pleased. Qiukai never showed any anger.

At last, Zihua's followers grew tired of entertaining themselves with this charade, and they took the old man to the top of a tower. One of them said to the rest of the crowd: "We will reward anyone with one hundred pieces of gold if he can throw himself off this tower." Everyone shouted for someone else to do it. Qiukai believed these words and jumped. He wafted like a bird and landed on the ground unharmed.

Zihua's followers thought that this was some fluke and did not think that anything was amiss. So they next went to a river bend where they pointed and said, "A precious pearl is at the bottom and you can grab it just for the diving." Qiukai again followed what they said, dove in, and surfaced with the pearl.

It began to dawn on the crowd that something was strange. Zihua had watched all this, and he ordered his servants to pile up expensive meats, foods, and bolts of silk brocade. He ordered a fearful ring of fire built around the mound. Then he said to Qiukai, "If you can walk through those flames, you can keep whatever you can carry as your reward." With no change to the color in his cheeks, Qiukai walked through the fire and came back with his arms full—and with no soot or burns on his body.

Zihua and his followers realized that Qiukai was one with the Tao, and they rushed to apologize. "We did not know that you had Tao and we acted childishly. We did not understand that you were supernatural and we dared to insult you. How stupid, deaf, and blind we were! But may we venture to ask how you have Tao?"

"I have no Tao," replied Qiukai. "Even in my heart, I know nothing. This is all I can tell you: A short time ago, two travelers stayed in my hut. I heard of Mr. Fan Zihua's reputation and influence, how he had the power of life and death, and how he could decide between wealth and ruin. I sincerely believed all this without a doubt. Since it wasn't that far, I decided to come here. Once I arrived, I believed everything that people said, and I was only afraid that I might never have any chance for success. I was so intent that I did not think of my own body or of good or harm. My mind was completely made up and nothing seemed to stop me. That was all.

"But now that I know what you really thought of me, my insides are filled with doubt. I know that I must watch and listen better. When I chased after good fortune, I was neither burned or drowned. Now just to think of that fire makes me hot inside and tremble with fear. How would I ever go near water or fire again?"

From that time on, when the followers of Fan Zihua happened to meet a beggar or horse doctor, they no longer bullied them. They would even dismount their chariots and bow in salute.

Zai Wo, a disciple of Confucius, heard this story, and asked about it. Confucius replied: "Don't you know? When

people have complete belief, they can feel everything including the movements of heaven and earth. They can see both ghosts and spirits, cross any of the six directions without trouble, and walk through the highest and narrowest of mountain paths. How then could entering water or fire be any trouble? Shang Qiukai had complete belief in what was made up—imagine what would be possible if a person was in accord with everyone else and had real sincerity? Little one—you must understand this!" (L)

69 | Concentrating Aims

When the ancient kings were faced with great tasks, they rid themselves of everything that might interfere with them. Thus they were certain to achieve their goals and eliminate what they did not want. In this way, they established their reputations and their accomplishments.

This is not true of ordinary leaders. When they have a great task, they are unable to rid themselves of everything that might interfere with them. Thus, they are unable to achieve their goals.

The difference between the worthy and the unworthy is that one can eliminate interference while the other cannot.

When a buck runs at top speed, a horse cannot catch up to it. But the deer will eventually be caught because it is always turning its head to look back.

A thoroughbred can cover a thousand kilometers in a day if it's pulling a light carriage. If the carriage is heavy, the horse cannot go more than a few kilometers.

I have never heard of a lack of effort among the worthy. But if some eminent people never achieved any benefit for the world, it was because they were pulling the stupid and unworthy. (LBW)

70 | Taming Tigers

King Xuan's zookeeper was named Liang Yang. He was marvelously skilled at raising wild birds and beasts. Whenever there was a feeding inside the king's park, every sort of animal—whether tigers, wolves, eagles, or osprey—ate in peace. Throughout the year, males and females mated freely, their offspring were plentiful, and all the species lived together without attacking one another.

The king was afraid that Liang's skills might be lost with him, so he ordered him to reveal his techniques. In response, Liang said, "I am merely a lowly servant. What art could I possibly show you? I have so little to say that I am afraid that your majesty will think that I am hiding something. However, I can tell you of my approach to raising tigers.

"All living creatures want to be happy and become angry when frustrated. Isn't it wong to ignore this point when taking care of any creature?

"When feeding tigers, I never give them live game; if they were to kill, it would excite them to rage. I do not give them whole sides of animals; tearing the bodies apart would again raise their tempers. Instead, I time how long it takes for them to get hungry, make sure they eat their fill regularly. I see whatever makes them ferocious and avoid it.

"Tigers and people may be different, but if both are treated well, they will become meek. They can't be controlled if they're allowed to kill. I had to find the way to overcome their anger. I had to be sure that they would follow what I wanted them to do, that they would have no need for rage, and that they would instead be rewarded with the happiness they naturally wanted. There could be no in-between.

"Now I don't have to use conscious force to control them. I simply watch the birds and the beasts enjoying each others' company. I let them wander in the park. They have no hankering for the high forests or the broad valleys, and they willingly return to their dens and roosts. If they do not long for the deep mountains or the quiet gorges anymore, it is only because of all that has been planned." (L)

71 | The Clever Daughter-In-Law

In olden times, a woman married into her husband's family and rarely saw her own family again. There happened to be an old man who had three sons. The two oldest were married and the daughters-in-law were devoted to the old man, but they sometimes wanted to go home to see their own mothers in distant towns. These visits meant that no one was there to take care of the old man for many days and this bothered him. The next time that the two women asked, he said, "I will give my permission this time, but unless you bring back two presents for me, I won't allow it again."

The two women asked what those two things were.

"One of you must bring me wind wrapped in paper and the other must bring me fire wrapped in paper."

The two quickly agreed without any thought and went off to see their mothers. But when it was time to return, they remembered the two gifts that they had promised to bring. Not knowing how to meet their father-in-law's request, they became increasingly somber.

On the road they met a simple country girl riding a water buffalo who asked about their glum expressions. They told her their story.

"Oh, that's easy," said the country girl. "Just bring the old man a fan and a lantern."

They went home in delight and surprised their father-in-law with his riddles solved. In time, they told him about the country girl.

The old man said: "I must have her for my daughter-in-law!" He sent matchmakers to find the country girl and arranged for her to marry his youngest son.

The old man had been wise. His new daughter-in-law was more intelligent than anyone in the household. Under her clever management, the family grew wealthy and happy. This made the old man so proud that he wrote an inscription that read, "No Sorrow," which he hung over the gate of the family home.

Not long after, a passing official was enraged to see such an inscription. He descended from his sedan chair and huffed, "Impudence! Nobody is free from sorrow." He had his guard summon the head of this foolish family to explain.

The third daughter-in-law came out to greet him instead of the old man.

"This is such an arrogant inscription," shouted the official. "I shall penalize your family to weave me a piece of cloth as long as this road!"

"Yes, your excellency. As soon as you find the two ends of this road and give me its length, I shall weave it for you."

The official was tongue-tied at first. Then he said, "I shall fine you as much oil as there is water in the sea."

"Surely. As soon as you tell me how many liters of water are in the sea, I shall press our beans for you."

The official's face turned red. "You, a mere woman, think you're so smart. All right. I won't fine you. But can you match my mind? Imagine that I hold a bird in my hand. Will I squeeze it to death or let it go?"

She replied instantly. "You, sir, are a high official and are surely smarter than a poor country woman. Perhaps, then, you can tell me that if I stand in this doorway with one foot inside and the other outside whether I intend to go in or out."

The official was stunned. Seizing on this moment, the third daughter-in-law said: "If your excellency cannot solve my riddle, you should not make me solve yours!"

The official said no more but climbed back into his sedan chair and went away. (FT)

72 | Do Not Oppress Hearts

Cui Ji said to Laozi: "If you do not govern the world, how will you pacify the hearts of the people?"

"You must be careful," said Laozi. "Do not oppress people's hearts. Discouraged hearts fall. Encouraged hearts rise. Once a heart plummets from high to low, it can be trapped in angry thoughts.

"The heart can be flowing and compliant. It can deal softly with the hard and strong, or it can be stiff and sharp enough to cut jade. It can be hot as scorching fire, or cold as solid ice. It can be fast enough to crouch or jump within seconds, or it can spread calmly beyond the four seas. It can come to rest, as still as a deep abyss, or it can buck and kick and balk at being tied. Such is the human heart!" (Z)

73 | Vulgar People

Vulgar people favor those like themselves, and they reject those who are different. They are partial to those whom they like, and they are indifferent to those with whom they differ. When they do that, they put themselves outside the hearts of the greater population.

But why do they separate themselves from others like that? Why won't they listen quietly to others? Why do they think that other people have few abilities?

When they take power over a nation, these vulgar people will demand benefits for themselves worth three kings, and they overlook the suffering that they cause. They govern the state by chance and luck, but how much could chance and luck destroy a state?

Not once in ten thousand times will the vulgar preserve the people's country. Once they have ruined a nation, not once in ten thousand times will there be anything left worth saving. It's terrible that the rulers of the lands don't know this! (Z)

74 | The Death of Primal Chaos

Brevity was the king of the Southern Sea. Suddenness was the king of the Northern Sea. Primal Chaos was the king of the Center. Brevity and Suddenness met often in Primal Chaos's land, and he was always good to them.

Brevity and Suddenness asked each other how they might repay Primal Chaos's hospitality. They reasoned, "All people have seven openings so that they can see, hear, eat, and breathe, but he alone has none. Let's try and drill them for him."

So each day, they drilled a hole.

And on the seventh day, Primal Chaos died. (Z)

75 | Finding the Right Spot

The state of Qi appointed Viscount Zhang to lead an alliance with the Han and Wei clans to attack the state of Jing. Jing appointed Tang Mie to command its armies.

The two armies camped on opposite shores of the Bi River, but had still not fought after six months. Eventually, the state of Qi ordered Viscount Zhang to begin the war at once.

The viscount responded: "Execution, death, the extermination of one's family—all of these a king can ordain for a subject. But he cannot tell me to battle when I should not, nor tell me to stop a battle when I should fight."

Viscount Zhang sent a scout to find where to ford the river, but the Zhu army shot at the man and made it impossible for him to fulfill his mission. A farmer who was mowing hay nearby said: "It's easy to know where to ford the river. Just look at where the Jing soldiers have posted the greatest number of guards. That is where the water is shallow. Where you see few sentries is where the water is deepest."

The scout took the farmer to see Viscount Zhang who rewarded him with delight. That night, the viscount sent troops to attack where Jing had the greatest number of guards. Tang Mie was killed.

Viscount Zhang was called one who knew how to be a general. (LBW)

76 | The Speech of King Kang

King Kang came forth and stood inside the palace gate. The Grand Guardian led the princes of the west in a procession from the left side of the gate, while the Duke of Bi led the princes of the east from the right. Each side paraded teams of light bay horses, all of which had manes and tails dyed red. Each prince raised a jade piece representing their rank and they presented gifts, pledging: "To a one, we will each protect the throne and offer the bounty of our territories." Each one kowtowed twice by touching their heads to the ground. The king, as rightful successor to the throne, solemnly bowed in return.

King Kang said: "Oh lords of many states, of Hou, Dian, Nan, and Wei, I address you in person. In the past, the Kings Wen and Wu were righteous and they unerringly enriched the people. They established justice, order, and trust and were the most illustrious rulers in all the world. Their officers were as courageous as bears, their ministers were never divided in their hearts, and they preserved the royal house. They followed the commands of god, and the heavenly ruler bestowed Tao on them and gave them land in all directions.

"Thus they established the states and protected the throne for all who came after them. Now I ask each of you to continue what your predecessors rendered to my predecessors. While you may live great distances away, let your hearts be with the royal house. Join solemnly with me so that I, a little child, will not be shamed!" (BD)

77 | Dedicating Everyone to Love

Hui Ang, a wandering teacher, went to visit King Kang, hoping to provide advice. After listening a little while to him, the king stamped his foot and rasped angrily: "This royal person likes courage and might. Don't talk of benevolence and righteousness! What can you, a stranger, teach me?"

"I have a way," replied Hui Ang, "Whereby a man, though courageous and mighty, will do no harm by a sword thrust or by hitting. Would your majesty be interested in this?"

"Good! I would like to hear about that!"

"Normally, if a man's sword does not pierce and if he hits no target, it is considered shameful. But I have a way for a man to be brave without needing the boldness to stab, and to be mighty without needing the boldness to hit. He will not be reckless, but neither will he be passive.

"People who lack the right intentions from the beginning, or warriors who have no right intentions at all, will have neither love nor goodness in their hearts. I propose that every man, woman, and child in the empire willingly dedicate themselves to love and to do good for others. That would be a virtue greater than courage and might, and it would be greater than all social distinctions. Would your majesty be interested in such an idea?"

"This royal person has long wanted to hear such an idea."

"It is nothing more than the teachings of Confucius and Mozi (470–391 BCE). Neither were princes and yet they were royal in stature. They held no rank and yet they were leaders. All the men, women, and children of the empire used to crane their necks and stand on tiptoe to get a glimpse of them because they wanted see the teachers who could bring peace and happiness to everyone. Now, your majesty is the lord of ten thousand chariots. If you are sincere in your purpose, all the people within the four borders of your realm will benefit, and the fame of your virtue would exceed Confucius or Mozi!"

King Kang of Song was quiet, and Hui Ang quickly withdrew. The king looked around at his courtiers and said, "Such high words from that stranger!" (L)

78 | Emperor Yao

In ancient times, Emperor Yao was a reverent, intelligent, cultured, thoughtful, and gentle ruler. He was sincere, courteous, and yielding. His brilliance extended to all four quarters, and he set standards from high to low. He brought regulation to all people, and all of them became intelligent. He united and harmonized the many vassal states. The people were transformed and it was a time of concord.

The emperor commanded the brothers Xi and He to observe the sky carefully and to calculate the motions of the sun, moon, and stars, along with the revolving divisions of the sky. He ordered Xi Zhong to move to Bright Valley in the east, to greet the rising sun and set the calendar. During that season, the days were of medium length and the star Niao signaled mid-spring. The people were in the fields, and the birds and the beasts mated.

He commanded Xi Shu to move to the Brilliant Capital in the south, to set the timing of the summer, and to observe the period of longest days. During that season, the days were at their longest and the star Huo signaled mid-summer. The people were the most active, and the feathers of birds and the fur of beasts thinned as their coats changed.

He sent He Zhong to move to Dark Valley in the west, to watch where the sun set, and to adjust the times of the harvest work in autumn. During that season, the nights were of medium length and the star Xu signaled mid-autumn. The people were at ease and the coats of the birds and the beasts were sleek.

He ordered He Shu to move to the Secluded Capital in the north, to understand the beginning and phases of winter. During that season, the days were at their shortest and the star Mao signaled mid-winter. The people stayed in their houses, and the coats of birds and beasts grew downy and thick.

Emperor Yao said to the brothers Xi and He: "A year consists of 366 days. By means of a leap month, we can fix the four seasons and know a complete year. This is how we will grant and manage the numerous kinds of work to be done in the empire and how we will make all our accomplishments."

Toward the end of his reign, the emperor said to the Official of the Four Mountains: "I have been on the throne for seventy years. You have carried out my orders well. Let me resign my place to you."

The official said, "I lack the virtue and would disgrace the title."

"Then show me someone, whether revealing them from among the illustrious or naming someone from the scattered and poor." (BD)

79 | No Use Trying to Rule the World

Emperor Yao proposed abdicating to Xu You (c. 2356–2255 BCE), the great recluse of the Ying River, saying: "When the sun and moon are in the sky, the flame of our torches is not needed. If the rains fall but we continue to irrigate the fields, our labors are not needed. Likewise, since you stand here as a ruler who could govern well, my shortcomings are obvious. I am also unneeded, and there is no reason for me to continue my rule. Please take the throne."

Xu You said: "You are already the ruler of the state and you govern well. If I were to take your place, wouldn't I only be doing so for the name? A name is merely the guest of the truth. Why should I be such a guest?

"When a tailorbird builds a nest, it uses just one branch. When a mole drinks from the river, it drinks just enough to fill its belly. Go back and forget this thought. I have no use for ruling the world.

"A cook may not run his kitchen perfectly, and yet the priest and the ceremonial representative of the dead do not knock over wine cups and wooden stands to take his place." (Z)

80 | Those Who Possess Land

Those who possess land hold everything. Those who hold everything should not treat things as if they are without substance—because if something wasn't substantial, it would not be a real thing. Understand this: that the substance of things cannot be taken for granted. How else can one person rule the world and the one hundred clans if this isn't understood?

Of all who come and go wherever they are, of all who travel throughout every region, of those who depart or those who arrive, of those who have little or those who have much—the ruler alone is responsible for them all. Only that can be called worthy. (Z)

81 | Making Use of a Fake Eunuch

When the First Emperor grew older, his empress carried on a secret affair with the chancellor, Lu Buwei (290–236 BCE). Apprehensive of being discovered, Buwei searched out Lao Ai, a man with an enormous penis, and made him his retainer. He had Lao Ai parade around with a wooden wheel hung from his penis, and he made sure that the empress heard the rumors. This inflamed her, and she wanted the man for herself.

Buwei suggested that they could pretend Lao Ai was a eunuch and that she could then take him into the palace. The two of them bribed the officers in charge of castration. They even plucked Lao Ai's eyebrows and beard to make him better look the part.

The empress delighted in Lao Ai and she soon became pregnant. She arranged for a false divination that told her to move to another palace—where Lao Ai was her constant attendant. She showered him with gifts, let him make decisions for her, and she gave him several thousand household slaves and a thousand retainers.

But the First Emperor soon heard rumors and he ordered an investigation. The officials discovered that Lao Ai was not a real eunuch, that the empress had borne two illicit sons, and that the pair had plotted to replace the emperor with one of their sons. Lu Buwei was also implicated.

Lao Ai took the empress's seal of authority and led an army to attack the palace. But the emperor's army rebuffed him. He fled. The warriors caught up to him, beheaded him, and the First Emperor ordered three generations of Lao Ai's entire clan wiped out. Lu Buwei's downfall followed.

The Grand Historian commented: Confucius would have described Lu Buwei as the sort of man who should have had a great reputation, but who was brought down by his own shortcomings. (RH)

82 | Once There Is Pervasiveness

Only heaven and earth are great, and all transformations are completed evenly because of them. Although the ten thousand things are numerous, they are ordered as one. In the same way, the legions of people are plentiful, but they are ruled by one emperor.

The source of the emperor's virtue must be completely with heaven. Thus it is said that the sublime ancients ruled by nonaction—simply through heaven's virtue rather than their own.

If we use Tao to examine their words, we see that the emperor of the world had to remain correct. If we use the Tao to examine the separation of minister and ruler, we can see that everyone had to be just and clear. If we use the Tao to examine the officials, we see that they had to be capable. If we use the Tao to examine the ten thousand things overall, we see that everything is as it ought to be—perfect.

Therefore, virtue is what pervades heaven and earth. Tao moves the ten thousand things. Skill is used to govern people, to conduct business, and to give proficiency and competence.

Skill should be a part of all matters. All matters should be joined with justice. All justice should be united with virtue. All virtue is united with Tao. Tao is united with heaven.

So it is said: "The ancients cultivated the world without their own desires, and the world had enough. They did nothing and the ten thousand things continued their evolution.

They were deeply calm and the one hundred clans remained settled."

"Once there is pervasiveness, ten thousand matters can be concluded. When a state of nonintention is reached, even the ghosts and spirits will obey." (Z)

83 | The Tao Spreads Over All

The master said: "The Tao covers and supports everything. It is overflowing in its greatness!

"The cultivated person should not hollow out their hearts to that fact.

"The meaning of heaven is to act through nonaction. The meaning of virtue is nonaction in speech. The meaning of benevolence is to love all people and to be good to all beings. The meaning of greatness is for all that is not alike to be joined. The meaning of vastness is to move where it is neither dangerous nor strange. The meaning of abundance is to hold ten thousand diversities. The meaning of the thread of life is to keep virtue. The meaning of establishment is the fixing of virtue. The meaning of perfection is accord with Tao. The meaning of completion is to keep anyone from grinding down the rights of another.

"When the cultivated person understands these ten points, they are restrained in all matters, they keep their hearts wide, and they let abundance pass to all beings.

"As such, let buried gold stay in the mountain, leave pearls sunken in the depths. Don't try to profit from goods and wealth, don't chase possessions and riches, don't rejoice in longevity, don't regret past youth, don't glory in being expert, don't be ashamed of hardship.

"Forget about longevity and youth, or hardship or being expert, or not enough talking. Don't grab the whole world for your own benefit or try to keep it for yourself. Don't try to rule the world as if it's your own private and self-evident domain. What should be self-evident should be understanding that all beings make a single treasury—and that life and death form a single condition." (Z)

84 | The Brilliant Tao

The master said: "The Tao: how deep it remains! How limpid is its purity!

"Metal and stone cannot call to you, even though metal and stone can make musical tones. They can't answer your questions. They can't even make the cries of birds or animals.

"What sets those differences between the ten thousand things apart?

"Those people with magnificent qualities pass with simplicity and humility in all matters. They have their root in the source of pervasive wisdom and spirituality. They have a vast, lifelong virtue, and when their hearts go forth, they gather everything.

"Form without Tao is not alive. Life without virtue is not brilliant. If form were to exist without life and be placed amid established virtue and the brilliant Tao, it would lose all its splendid qualities.

"Overwhelming! Suddenly issuing forth in overpowering movement so all things must follow: such are called those with magnificent virtue. They can see into the deepest darkness, hear where there are no sounds, look into the depths of obscurity and see as clear as dawn. They can also hear harmony in the midst of noise.

"Thus, even in extremes upon extremes, they can find substance. Where there is the ethereal upon the ethereal, they can discern the essence.

"In this way, they can connect with all the ten thousand things and arrive in a place where there is no want and no need, no times of hurry nor of halting—no matter how big or small, long or short, near or far." (Z)

85 | The Teaching of the Great Person

A great person's teaching is as quick as a shadow's shape or an echo's sound. They answer each question instantly, exhausting all that they carry in their breast and matching all that they know of the world.

They are silent in rest; unrestricted in movement; modest in finding the right resolution. They roam without end; come and go without parallel. They are as beginningless as the sun. With admirable form and presence, their teachings combine in a grand fusion.

Such a great person is never selfish. They don't covet and are not possessive, and they are equal to the cultivated persons of classical times.

When you see such openness, look carefully: there is the friend of heaven and earth. (Z)

86 | Seizing Opportunity

Wu Qi ruled River West and wanted to prove to his citizens that he would keep his promises. He ordered a pole planted outside the south gate and issued an edict that anyone who could knock it down would be given the rank of superior grand officer.

No one tried from morning to night of the next day. They all said, "This certainly can't be believed."

Finally one man said, "I'll try. The worst that can happen is that I won't get the reward, so what's the harm?" He knocked the pole down and went to see Wu Qi. After checking himself, Wu Qi made the man a superior grand officer.

That evening Wu Qi had another pole planted and he issued the same edict. This time, the townspeople fought with each other to knock the pole down, but it was more firmly planted than before. No one succeeded.

From that time on, the people believed in Wu Qi's word.

When offers of reward and punishment are accepted by the people, how could any undertaking, even military ones, not succeed? (LBW)

Yu Rang (c. 450 BCE) of Jin was a minister of the Fan and Zhongxing clans. But he felt that he was not advancing in life, and he left to join Zhi Bo (d. 453 BCE) and his clan. Zhi valued him greatly and treated him with high honor.

The Zhi armies destroyed the Houses of Fan and Zhongxing. After that, Zhi Bo launched an attack on Viscount Zhao Xiangzhi (d. 425 BCE), who fought back with an alliance of the Zhao, Wei, and Han Clans. They annihilated the House of Zhi, killed Zhi Bo, and divided the Zhi lands between themselves. Zhao Xiangzi hated Zhi Bo so much that he had his skull made into a drinking cup.

Yu Rang fled to the mountains and vowed: "Alas, a gentleman must be willing to die for one who appreciated him as much as a lover appreciating a beautiful woman. Zhi Bo honored me. I must avenge him, even at the risk of my own death. If I cannot make an honorable report to Zhi Bo, I will be disgraced to my very soul."

He changed his name and became a servant in the palace. Smuggling a dagger with him, he waited in a privy for a chance to stab Xiangzi. But Xiangzi had a suspicion and ordered his soldiers to search. They found Yu Rang and discovered the dagger.

"I am here to avenge Zhi Bo," Yu Rang said.

The soldiers around him wanted to kill him where he stood. But Xiangzi said, "Here is a righteous man. I tried to make sure no one was left after Zhi Bo, and yet this minister wants to avenge him. He must be one of the most virtuous men in the world."

He ordered his soldiers to let Yu Rang go.

In the months that followed, Yu Rang made scars and sores all over his body with lacquer and swallowed charcoal to make his voice hoarse. In order to disguise himself completely, he became a beggar in the marketplace. Even his wife could not recognize him.

But once, a friend did notice him. "Aren't you Yu Rang?"

"I am."

"You're a person of great talent. Why don't you try to serve under Xiangzi? You would surely advance in his favor, and then you'd be close enough to fulfill your purpose. Why mutilate yourself and suffer so much just to take revenge on Xiangzi? This approach is much too hard!"

"If I were to enter into his service and kill him, I would be guilty of disloyalty to him as my lord. This way may be of the utmost difficulty, but I will shame any future generations who would be disloyal to their lords."

One day, Yu Rang hid under a bridge. When Xiangzi's entourage reached the crossing, the horses shied away, and Xiangzi said, "Yu Rang must be here!"

He ordered his soldiers forward. They fanned out and they found Yu Rang. Xiangzi confronted Yu Rang. "You once served the Houses of Fan and Zhongxing. But when Zhi Bo exterminated them, you continued to serve him and did not try to avenge your former lords. Why then should you be so determined to avenge Zhi Bo's death?"

"When I served the Houses of Fan and Zhongxing, they treated me as an ordinary man, and I responded to them in an ordinary way. But Zhi Bo treated me with supreme respect as the highest person in the nation and so I am obligated to repay him in the same way."

Xiangzi sighed and wept. "Oh Yu Rang! Your loyalty to Zhi Bo is admirable! I already let you go once. Now you must fix this yourself. I will not release you again." At that, the soldiers closed in on Yu Rang.

Yu Rang said: "I have heard that a wise master will not conceal the abilities of those who serve him, and a loyal subject will die to be known for righteousness. Once, you were generous in sparing me and the whole world heard of your virtue. I am ready to be punished today, but I ask you to let me strike your robe so I can say that I fulfilled my vow. Once that's done, I will die content. It is presumptuous of me to dare ask, but I beg you to grant my request."

Moved by Yu Rang's righteousness, Xiangzi took off his robe and ordered it handed over. Yu Rang unsheathed his sword, leapt at the robe, and pierced it three times. "Now I can go down to face Zhi Bo," he cried. Then he fell on his own sword. The news of his death made all the men of the nation weep. (RH)

88 | Fire Mountain

Zhao Xiangzi led 100,000 men to hunt in the mountains. Lighting the dry weeds, they set the whole forest on fire, and the glow could be seen for a hundred kilometers around. Suddenly, a man came out of the rocky cliff and climbed down through the smoke and flying embers. Everyone thought he must have been supernatural.

The fire roared behind him, but he walked calmly forward without any sign of trouble. Xiangzi was amazed and examined the man carefully. He certainly looked human in shape and color. He had the seven openings of eyes, ears, nostrils, and mouth, and he breathed and made sounds when he moved just like any other man. "How did you come out of the rock?" Xiangzi asked. "How could you walk through fire?"

The man replied: "What do you mean by 'rock'? What do you mean by 'fire'?"

"Why, you just came out of the rock and climbed down. You just walked through fire."

"I don't know what those things are."

Marquis Wen of Wei (d. 369 BCE) heard of this story and asked Zixia, a student of Confucius, about it. "What kind of man was that?"

Zixia said, "My master told me that when a man of great harmony knows no difference between himself and everything else, then nothing can hurt him or stop him. Passing through metal or rock, dancing through water or fire—anything is possible." (L)

89 | The Wise Judge

Once, two poor women appeared before a judge, each one claiming to be the mother of an infant boy.

One woman declared: "This child is mine!"

The other shouted in return: "No, he's mine!"

The judge silenced them both and cast about for a way to resolve the situation. Finally, he thought of a solution and said: "Each of you claims this boy as your own. I can hardly order him cut in half to give to each of you. Instead, I offer to adopt him myself. I guarantee that I will bring him up to be a great scholar and wealthy official."

One woman remained silent. The other insisted that she still wanted the boy.

The judge gave the child to the silent woman. He knew that she would have taken the opportunity for the boy to become the greatest possible success in the empire, even if that meant giving him up. The false mother objected because she only wanted the boy for herself. (FT)

90 | Confucius and the Weeping Woman

Once, Confucius and his disciples were traveling near Mount Tai when they came upon a woman, bent over a fresh grave, and weeping terribly. Confucius sent one of his pupils, Zilu, to inquire.

"Madam, you wail as if you suffered great sorrow."

"I live in this district," the woman sobbed. "One tiger killed my father-in-law. Then another killed my husband. And now, a third one has killed my son."

Confucius arrived by this point and asked her, "Why don't you leave this place?"

"This district has no corrupt government here."

Confucius was taken aback, and told his disciples: "Little ones, remember this: a corrupt government is crueler than tigers." (BR)

91 | The Tao of Swimming

Confucius and his disciples were walking in the wilderness when they found a waterfall that was thirty fathoms high and that stirred up frothing rapids thirty kilometers long. Turtles, alligators, and fish could not even swim in the rough waters.

They witnessed a lone figure dive from the top of the cliff into the turbulent pool. Thinking that a man was trying to kill himself, Confucius ordered his students to rush to the rescue. But by the time the disciples had run the hundred meters, the man had climbed nonchalantly onto the bank and was sitting beside some crabapple trees. He spread his hair out to dry in the sun and was singing happily.

By this time, Confucius arrived and asked: "I saw you dive, and I thought you wanted to end your life in rapids so rough that even turtles, alligators, and fish could not swim in it. Yet you not only dived and swam, you climbed out singing. At first, I thought you must have been a supernatural creature. But now that I am close to you, I can see that you are a man. May I ask how you could swim in such dangerous waters? What Tao do you have?"

"Oh no! I have no Tao! I merely start from the Origin, I fulfill my nature, and I am complete in my fate. When I swim, I commit myself wholeheartedly from the start, as if offering everything I am with both hands, and then I swim swiftly and regularly until I climb back out. The Tao of swimming is the secret of being effortless. Only in this way might I be said to have Tao."

"How is it possible for a person to start from the Origin, fulfill their nature, and be complete in their fate?"

"If I were born in the mountains, then I would be content in the mountains. In my case, I was born near this waterfall, so I am content in this waterfall. Our inner natures are the same way. Whatever I don't know isn't part of my natural situation. All life is the same." (L)

92 | King Mu and the Magician

During the time of King Mu, a magician came to the court from the far west. He could enter fire or water, penetrate metal and stone, overturn mountains and reverse rivers, move whole cities and counties, ride on air without falling, and could not be stopped by any object. He could generate a thousand changes and transformations without running out and, besides being able to change the shape of anything, he could also ease anyone's worries.

King Mu treated him like a god and served him as if he were a prince. He offered the magician a spacious suite of apartments, sacrificed three animals to welcome him, and chose singing girls for the magician's pleasure.

The magician, however, said that the palace was much too low and inferior a place for him to live, the food was too rancid to serve at any banquet, and the concubines were too smelly and ugly to touch.

So King Mu ordered a new palace built with many floors. The builders used only the finest brick and wood, painted the walls and columns in gorgeous red and white, and finished every detail with remarkable skill. Five royal treasuries were emptied by the time the final tower was done. The palace stood eight thousand meters high, was taller than Mount Zhongnan, and was named the Tower that Touches the Sky. The king filled the palace with maidens from Zheng and Wei. They were exquisitely beautiful, anointed with fragrant perfume, lovely with their moth-eyebrows, bejeweled with hairpins and earrings, and dressed in the finest silks with the richest satin trains. Their faces were powdered, their eyebrows darkened, and they were adorned with jade. Each room was filled with sweetly scented plants and delightful music. Every month, the magician was offered luxurious clothing. Every morning, he was served new and delicious food.

The magician could not well refuse to live in this palace. But he had not stayed long before he invited the king to accompany him on a trip. So the king clutched the magician's sleeve and soared up with him into the sky, until at last they reached the magician's own palace.

This palace was built with beams of gold and silver and its walls were encrusted with pearls and jade. It towered high above the mists and rain on unseen foundations like a city in the clouds. The sights and sounds it offered to eye and ear, and the scents and flavors which abounded there were far more exquisite than anything the wealthiest of men knew. The king thought he was in a paradise of azure clouds, a true part of heaven filled with happiness, the very dwelling of the gods themselves. He looked down on his own palace, and it seemed no more than a pile of clods and brushwood. The king lingered in the palace for several decades without giving any thought to his own kingdom.

Then the magician invited him to take another journey, and they came to a place where neither the sun nor moon could be seen above, nor any rivers or seas seen below. The light was stunningly bright. The king was confused and he could not see anything. The sounds were so loud and strange that he could not hear. His bones and organs rattled and seized up, his mind was scattered, and his very essence was lost. He begged the magician to take him back. The magician gave him a shove, and the king felt himself plummet through empty space.

When he woke, he found himself sitting on his own throne as before, with the same attendants around him. He looked at the wine in front of him—its sediment had not settled. He looked at the meal set before him: it had not been tasted. He asked where he had just come from, but his attendants replied that he had simply been sitting there. This threw the king into a three-month period of disquiet.

Finally, he summoned the magician for an explanation.

The magician gave this explanation: "Your majesty and I were traveling as spirits. How could our bodies move? Did we really go from here to a different palace? Did we really travel beyond your own grounds? You are distracted, doubting the difference between the permanent and the fleeting. Transformation and change occur to the utmost. Yet you sit there, sick with your musings, unable to tell what is real."

The king was greatly intrigued by this talk at first, but his interest in the affairs of state gradually ebbed. He no longer spent any time with his officials or his concubines. Finally, he decided to go on a long journey. He ordered a chariot drawn by eight steeds. Each horse was a different color, and each one was famous for its excellence.

King Mu called his driver and they embarked on a trip of thousands of kilometers. They journeyed on until they came to a country of tribesman. A huge crowd gathered and offered him the blood of a snow goose to drink, and they washed his feet with cow and mare's milk.

They continued on to the Kunlun Mountains, where the waters ran red in the setting sun and where he saw the palace of the Yellow Emperor himself. King Mu erected a stone stele in tribute so that future generations would know of the great Yellow Emperor.

Next he visited the Queen Mother of the West, who welcomed him with a banquet and the music of jade chimes. Together they sang a duet, but at the end of their song, King Mu grew pensive and melancholy.

As the sun set, he saw that he had journeyed ten thousand kilometers a day for naught. "As an individual, I did not fully keep my virtue," he sighed. "Instead, I threw myself into revelry and song. Where I should have been pursuing my destiny as a ruler, I fell into excess instead."

Among gods and people, how many great rulers have been able to reduce their own enjoyment to gain a hundred years of social advancement or to help the world rise above the false? (L)

93 | Mr. Yin's Illness

Mr. Yin owned a large estate where he harried his servants brutally, giving them no rest from morning to night. There was one old servant whose physical strength was almost gone, and yet Mr. Yin drove him to work harder. The old man groaned throughout the day as he worked, and when night came, he was so tired that he fell asleep right away.

Each night, his spirit wandered away from his body, and he dreamed that he was the king of an entire nation ruling people of his own. He took his pleasure in his palaces, followed his own whims in everything, and found no end to his happiness. But when he awoke, he was servant again.

When somebody tried to console him over his hard life, the old man replied: "A person may live one hundred years, with the whole divided equally into nights and days. By day, I am a slave and trapped in great bitterness. By night, I am a king with incomparable happiness. Why should I grumble?"

For his part, Mr. Yin's mind dwelled continuously on worldly cares; he was always concerned with the profits of his family's business. He wore out his body and mind, and each night he fell asleep with great fatigue. Every night he dreamed that he was another man's servant, running about endlessly and scolded and beaten constantly with canes. He muttered, moaned, and cried out in his sleep, and he slowly became deeply ill.

Mr. Yin went to a friend for advice. His friend told him: "You have a glorious station in life, and you have abundant property and wealth. You are far better off than nearly anyone else. If you dream at night that you are a slave suffering bitterness and hardship, that is only the situation becoming normal and balanced. You wish to combine the pleasures of your waking life with your dreams. But how could you do that?"

Mr. Yin listened to his friend. He lightened his servants' workload and put aside more time to relax and reduce his business worries. Slowly, his illness eased and he became calm. (L)

94 | The Gardener

Zigong, a student of Confucius, was traveling north of the Han River when he saw an old man working in a vegetable garden.

The old man had dug his furrows, gone to a well, and was bringing water back in a jar to pour into the ditches. He toiled and spent a great deal of energy, but he got little done.

Zigong said: "If you used equipment, you could soak a hundred fields in a day. You could achieve a great result with little effort. Would you like to try it, sir?"

The gardener looked up and asked: "How does it work?"

"It is a wooden lever, heavy behind, light in front. It draws the water as quickly as a pot boiling over. It is called a water pulley."

The gardener stood up in exasperation, then laughed. "I have heard my teacher say that where there are machines, there are sure to be machinations. Where there are machinations, there are sure to be scheming hearts. When pure simplicity is impaired, the living spirit is unsettled and cannot be with Tao. I know what you're referring to, but I would be ashamed to use it."

Zigong blushed, hung his head, and said no more. (Z)

95 | The Water Pulley

Have you seen a water pulley? Pull it and it goes down, release it, and it goes up. A person pulls it—it does not pull the person.

Whether it goes down or goes up, it never disobeys the person working it.

In the same way, the rites, conduct, laws, and standards of the Three Legendary Kings and the Five Great Emperors were impartial in bringing people together and ruling them. Those rulers might seem as different from one another as the flavors of hawthorns, pears, tangerines, and pomelos, and yet all of them nourished the people. (Z)

96 | Going to the Ocean

Zhun Mang was on his way to the ocean, when he met with Yuan Feng on the shore of the Eastern Sea.

"Where are you going, sir?" Yuan Feng asked.

"I am going to the ocean."

"What for?"

"Such is the nature of the ocean that streams and rivers flow into it but never fill it and the water that drains from it never exhausts it," replied Zhun Mang. "I will enjoy lingering there."

"Have you no thoughts about society? I would like to hear you speak about sagely government."

Zhun Mang said: "Under the government of sages, all officers are assigned without mistake according to the fitness of their natures; all appointments are made exactly according to the ability of each person; decisions are made after a complete survey of all opinions and matters; and actions and words proceed from inner impulses. The whole world is transformed. Wherever the sages point or glance, people from all directions are sure to go. That is what is called sagely government."

"I should like to hear about virtuous government."

"The virtuous leaders remain without thought; they act without worry; they don't store up what is wrong, good, or bad; they share benefit with everyone within the four seas and everyone says that they're satisfied; they give to all, and everyone says they're at peace. When they die, people grieve like children who have lost their mothers, and are confused like those who have lost their way. Yet when the citizens invest wealth, they have surplus and they don't even know where it comes from; they have enough food and drink and they don't know from where it follows. This is what is called the appearance of virtuous people."

"I should like to hear about those of high spirituality."

"Those of high spirituality ascend in brilliance, and they transcend bodily form. They are called shining and ethereal. Heaven and earth are tranquil and every matter is completed. The ten thousand things return to their true natures. That is what I call moving and deep." (Z)

97 | The Deer

There was a man in the state of Zheng who was gathering firewood in the wilds when he chanced upon a startled deer. The woodcutter managed to hit the deer and kill it. Fearful that someone else would find his treasure, he pulled the deer into a ditch and covered it with leaves. He was quite pleased with his good luck.

However, he soon forgot where he had hidden the deer, and he eventually thought it may all have been a dream. He told other people the story as he went about his work, and one of the people who heard him was able to figure out where the deer was hidden and he retrieved it later.

When this second man brought the deer home, he told his wife: "A woodcutter dreamed that he caught a deer, but he couldn't remember where he had left it. I found it. So that shows the dream was real."

"On the contrary," said his wife, "you must have dreamed that you met a woodcutter who had caught a deer. After all, where is the woodcutter? Yes, you really have a deer, but does that mean your dream really came true?"

"I've got the deer. What does it matter whether it was his dream or mine?"

In the meantime, the woodcutter had gone home, and at first, he didn't mind that he had lost the deer. But that night, he dreamed of the hiding place, and he also dreamed of the man who had taken the deer. The next morning, following his dream, he sought out the second man to get the deer back.

An argument broke out, and in the uproar the bystanders called the magistrate.

Once in court, the magistrate said to the woodcutter: "First you really captured a deer, but you foolishly spoke of your dream. The other person really got the deer, and now you're both fighting over it. Your wife, on the other hand, said a dream of a deer was not unusual, and for her, no one had a deer. Yet, we have a deer now. I order you to divide it between yourselves."

The case was reported to the King of Zheng, who said: "The magistrate must have dreamed of dividing the deer!"

Whereupon the prime minister commented, "What is a dream and what is not a dream? Officials can make no pronouncement to distinguish the two. If you want to know the difference between waking and dreaming, only the Yellow Emperor or Confucius could determine that. But both of them are long gone. So who can make such distinctions today? All we can do is follow the magistrate's decision." (L)

Yangli Huazi, a middle-aged man, fell into a state of forget-fulness. Anything he heard in the morning was forgotten by nightfall, and anything that happened at night was forgotten by morning. When he was outside, he forgot where he was going. When he was inside, he forgot to sit down. In the pres-ent, he forgot the past; later, he did not know how he had ar-rived at the present. His entire family was deeply troubled.

Fortune-tellers were hired, but their divining revealed nothing. Wizards were summoned, but their exorcisms had no effect. Doctors were called, but their treatments provided no cure.

Finally, a scholar from the state of Lu sent word through an intermediary that he knew a cure. Huazi's wife offered him half their estate if only he would help them. The scholar said: "This case cannot be cured by fortune-telling, omens, or divination. It cannot be cured by exorcisms or prayers. It cannot be cured by herbal or mineral potions. I must try to change his heart, and relieve what is bothering him no matter how extensive it may be. Only then can I cure him!"

The treatment began. The scholar exposed Huazi to the dewy cold until he begged for clothing, starved him until he asked for food, left him alone in the dark until he asked for light. Soon the scholar was able to report to Huazi's family with satisfaction:

"This disease can be cured. But my techniques have been handed down in secret through many generations and cannot be revealed to outsiders. All the servants must be sent away, and I must shut myself alone with the patient for seven days."

They did as he asked, and no one knew what happened during that week.

On the eighth morning, the illness of many years finally came to an end! Yangli Huazi was fully aware again.

But as soon as he regained his senses, he flew into a great rage. He drove his wife away, slapped his sons, and grabbed a spear to attack the scholar. The people of Song stopped him from committing any serious violence. They asked him what was wrong.

Huazi replied: "I had forgotten everything before. All was washed away, and I had no consciousness of the world's problems. Now I am aware again. I can remember the events of decades past. I know again of life and death, sadness and joy, good and bad. I'm tangled in ten thousand threads of disturbance and agitation. I have an overwhelming fear that my future will be a struggle between life and death, gain and loss, sadness and happiness, and good and bad. Oh, if only I could regain but a moment of my past forgetfulness!" (L)

99 | The Men Who Switched Hearts

Lu Gonghu and Zhao Qiying both got sick. They went to consult Bian Que (d. 310 BCE), who cured them both.

Once that was done, he said: "Your illnesses attacked from the outside in, and I was able to cure them with herbs and mineral medicines. However, both of you have inner illnesses that have been festering since your births. Should I try to address them as well?"

Before they agreed, they asked: "Tell us your proposals first."

Bian Que said to Gonghu: "Your will is strong, but your energy is weak. Thus, you have plenty of ideas, but your accomplishments fall short. Qiying, on the other hand, has a weaker will but his energy is strong. He has fewer concerns, but he blunders in simple actions. I propose to switch your hearts. Then all should be well-balanced."

Bian Que gave each man a sedating wine to drink, and they were unconscious for three days. He cut open their chests, switched their hearts, and then sewed them up with marvelous medical skill. When the two men awoke, they felt as they did before. They got up and returned home.

But strangely, Gonghu went to Qiying's house, where Qiying's wife and children naturally did not recognize him. In the meantime, Qiying went to Gonghu's house and that family did not recognize him either. The two families brought a lawsuit, and Bian Que was called before the judge. He explained what had happened and the lawsuit was settled. (L)

100 | A Jester's Wisdom

The First Emperor of Qin wanted to expand his imperial pleasure park deep into the Hangu Pass.

"A great idea, your majesty," said Chan, his jester. "Fill it with animals too! When invaders come, the stags can gore the enemy to death!"

The emperor abandoned the plan.

Later, his successor, the Second Emperor, wanted to lacquer the walls of his capital.

"Splendid!" Chan said. "If you had not issued this command, I would have proposed it myself. Perhaps it will cost the people dearly, but it will be so fine! No invader will be able to climb such beautiful and smooth walls. Besides, lacquer is so easy to apply—although every wall will need a larger shelter for the long curing process."

The Second Emperor burst out laughing and gave up the idea. (RH)

101 | The Robot

King Mu of Zhou made an inspection tour of the west. He crossed the Kunlun Mountains but turned back before he reached the Yan Mountains. On his return journey, a craftsman named Yanshih asked for an audience on the road. King Mu received him and asked, "What are you able to do?"

"Your subject can make anything you command," replied Yanshih. "But your subject has already made something that his majesty may want to see."

"Bring it with you tomorrow. My court and I will view it together."

The next day, Yanshih came again to pay his respects. Seeing a companion with him, King Mu asked, "Who is that with you?"

"Your subject has made this himself," said Yangshih of the figure standing beside him. The king was astonished to look at the robot. It could walk, bow, and raise its head. It could truly have been called a person. The craftsman touched the robot's chin, and it began to sing perfectly in tune. He touched its hand, and the robot danced with a lively rhythm. It demonstrated what seemed like a thousand movements and ten thousand variations—more than enough to impress anyone. The king, his noblemen, consort, and concubines could not look away.

As the demonstration drew to a close, the robot winked flirtatiously at the concubines. This angered King Mu, and he ordered the craftsman put to death. Yanshih was terrified, and he immediately pulled the robot to pieces to show that it was not real. Everyone could see that it was leather and wood glued together and painted with white, black, red, and green lacquer.

The king carefully inspected the pieces and found all the internal organs present—liver, gall, heart, lungs, spleen, kidneys, intestines, and stomach—all supported by bones with joints, encased in muscle, and covered with skin and hair. The robot even had teeth. While all of it was artificial, every single part had been meticulously finished. When the pieces were reassembled the figure looked the same as before.

When the king tried to take away the heart, he found that the mouth could not speak. When he took away the liver, the eyes could not see. When he took away the kidneys, the legs could not move.

Now the king was satisfied and he exclaimed: "Human ingenuity can really reach such a high level!" He commanded that a chariot be readied to bring the craftsman and the robot back home with him.

Up until that time, Banshu with his cloud ladder and Mozi with his flying kite thought themselves the ultimate craftsmen. But when their students told them of Yanshih's invention, they never again boasted of their accomplishments, and they spent far less time with their plans and rulers. (L)

102 | The Right Use

The philosopher Hui Shi said to Zhuangzi: "The King of Wei gave me the seeds for some large gourds. I planted them, and when the gourds were ripe, they were big enough to hold five stones. I filled one with water, but it was so heavy that I couldn't lift it by myself. I cut another in half to make ladles, but the shells didn't have the right shape. They were nothing but big useless things! So I broke them up."

"Sir, you are quite clumsy in dealing with big things," replied Zhuangzi. "You remind me of somebody from the state of Song who had a salve that protected hands from cold water and chapping. He came from a family that had bleached silk for generations and this was their treasure. A stranger heard of this and offered to buy the formula for one hundred ounces of gold. When the family met to consider the proposal, they said, 'We have bleached silk for generations and have never even seen any gold. Now, in one morning, we can sell our formula for one hundred ounces of gold. Let's agree!'

"The stranger left with the formula and told the King of Wu, who was at war with Yue at the time. The king gave the stranger command of his fleet. There was a great naval battle in the middle of winter. Since the soldiers had the salve, they had a great victory over Yue. As a result, the king gave a large piece of the captured territory to the stranger as a fief.

"Now, the salve's ability to protect from cold and chaffing was the same, but for one it led to a fief, and for the family it only let them keep bleaching silk. The difference came from how the salve was used.

"Now you, sir, had gourds big enough to hold five stones. Why didn't you make a raft out of them and drift on the rivers and lakes? Instead you got discouraged and thought they were useless for holding anything. Your mind, master, is all tangled!" (Z)

103 | What Is Called Tao?

What do we call Tao?

Let us compare the way of heaven and the way of humans.

Effortless and yet worthy of the highest reverence—that is the way of heaven. Effortful—that is the way of humans.

The way of heaven is kingly. The way of humans is lowly.

The way of heaven and the way of humans are far apart. You must not fail to look at this. (Z)

104 | Diversity and Unity

Using a finger to point to what-a-finger-is-not is not as good as using what-is-not-a finger to indicate what-a-finger-is-not. Using a horse to show what-a-horse-is-not is not as good as using what-is-not-a-horse to show what-a-horse-is-not.

Heaven and earth: one finger.

All creatures and all things: one horse.

Is that possible or impossible? A path forms by constant walking. Things are named until we agree that they are so. How could that not be so? It is not so because it is not so.

Everything is so. Everything is possible. Therefore, whether a stalk or a pillar, a leper or the great beauty Xi Shi (b. 506 BCE), the immense or the changeable, the grotesque or the strange, they are one in Tao.

There may seem to be separation and joining, completion and destruction, but in all things there is no actual completion or destruction—only an ongoing returning clear through to unity. (Z)

105 | Three in the Morning

Let us not take the ordinary view. In the ordinary view, everything must be useful. When we look for the practical, we want everything to be clear. When we are clear, we expect a conclusion. Once we have succeeded, we want a tally, and then we stop there. We look no further, without really knowing what is so, and yet we call that Tao. We have toiled to our souls trying to reach a single understanding and yet may have still failed to reach any accord. That's called, "three in the morning."

What is "three in the morning"?

A monkey keeper was giving out acorns and said, "I will give you three this morning, and then four this evening."

All the monkeys were mad.

"Very well," said the keeper. "Then I shall give you four this morning and three this evening."

All the monkeys were happy.

His proposals were no different, but one resulted in acceptance and the other in anger. That's the way it is. The sagely person harmonizes between yes and no, and relies on the equalizing power of heaven. That is called moving on two paths. (Z)

106 | What Is Death, Really?

Chang Wuzi said: "How do I know that delight in living is not an illusion? How do I know that dislike of death is like a young person getting lost and not knowing that they are really on their way home?

"The great beauty Li was from the land of Ai. When she was first captured by the country of Jin, she sobbed until the tears soaked her dress. But after she was brought to the royal palace, shared the same couch as the king, and ate his grass-fed meat, she regretted that she had wept. How do I know whether or not the dead regret their earlier lives?

"Those who dream of drinking rare wine may cry and wail the next morning. Those who dream of weeping and wailing may wake to go hunting the next morning. While they were dreaming, they may even have tried to understand their dream, but when they awoke, they definitely knew that they had been dreaming. What if there's a great awakening, after which we know this all to have been a big dream?" (Z)

107 | Penumbra and the Shadow

Penumbra asked the Shadow: "Once, you were moving. Now, you've stopped. Once you sat. Now you're standing up. Why are you so unstable?"

The Shadow said: "I must wait before I can follow! Then I have to wait and wait to follow some more! I am like the scales that depend on a snake or the wings that depend on a cicada. How would I know why that is? Or how would I know why it is not?" (Z)

108 | The Butterfly Dream

In the past, I, Zhuangzi, dreamed that I was a butterfly, happily flitting and fluttering here and there and doing as I pleased. I did not know that I was Zhuangzi.

Suddenly, I awoke and I was again Zhuangzi. I did not know whether I had been Zhuangzi, dreaming that he was a butterfly, or whether I was now a butterfly dreaming that he was Zhuangzi.

But between Zhuangzi and a butterfly, there must be some difference. This is called the transformation of things. (Z)

109 | Why Mourn?

When Laozi died, Qin Shi went to pay his respects. He cried out three times and then left. The disciples asked him, "Weren't you a friend of the master?"

"I was."

"To mourn the way you have—is that acceptable?"

"It is. I thought he was more than a man, but now I don't think so. When I entered to mourn, old men wailed as if they had lost their sons, and young men moaned as if they had lost their mothers. What had the master done to create such attachments? Surely there had been something unsaid that led these men to make so much noise. This was the result of the master hiding himself from heaven and repeatedly expressing his own feelings. He ignored what he received naturally in this life. The ancients called this 'trying to escape heaven's retribution.'

"One enters by chance. The master had his time here. One leaves by chance. The master had to go. One should best spend one's time peacefully while here and then leave. Neither grief nor joy should enter into it. The ancients called this 'loosening the bounds.'"

We are pointing at the ashes after the logs have already burned. The fire has already gone elsewhere, and we don't realize it's already gone. (Z)

110 | Do Not Assist Heaven

The sages of the past observed heaven but did not try to assist it. They tried to perfect their virtue without being elaborate. They went forth in accord with Tao without strategy. They were cordial when cooperating with others but never presumed. They upheld righteousness lightly and didn't try to hoard anything for themselves. They conformed to propriety without making it restrictive. They never refused to engage in any matter as it came. They made their laws fair and avoided turmoil. They believed in the people and were never careless with them. They gave all things their due without abandoning them and couldn't do enough for them.

Those who don't know how to work with heaven are not pure in their virtue. Those who are not connected with Tao have no course to follow. Those who don't understand Tao—tragic! (Z)

111 | Following Heaven and Earth

A long time ago, Shun questioned Yao: "How does an august ruler use his heart?"

"I don't abuse the helpless," replied Yao. "I don't neglect poor citizens. I grieve for the dead. I take joy in children and I support the widowed. That's how I use my heart."

"That may be beautiful, but it is not great."

"Then what would you have me do?"

"Heavenly virtue moves forth serenely. The sun and moon shine, the four seasons turn. Day and night follow their course. The clouds arrive and give rain."

"Oh, I see, and I will keep this with me! You, sir, want to be in accord with heaven, while I have only wanted to be in accord with people."

Now, the ancient people regarded heaven and earth as great. The Yellow Emperor, Yao, and Shun all found that beautiful. What did those former rulers of old have to do? They just had to be like heaven and earth. (Z)

112 | Losing Proper Nature

Take a block of a one-hundred-year-old tree and make a sacrificial vessel from it. Paint it green and yellow. Throw the waste wood into the dump.

Compare the sacrificial vessel with what's lying in the dump, and you might say that they differ in beauty and ugliness—but they have both lost their essential nature. (Z)

113 | Going Beyond Books

The world thinks that the most valuable words of Tao have been put in books, but books cannot surpass what is passed on by oral teaching.

Oral teaching has its value, but what is valuable in those words are the ideas.

Ideas should be understood, but the idea that is understood cannot be put into words. Therefore what the world most values cannot be passed on through books. (Z)

114 | The Wheelwright

Duke Huan was sitting in his hall reading a book, while Wheelwright Bian was carving wood outside. Laying aside his hammer and chisels, Bian bowed to the duke and said, "May I dare ask what the duke is reading?"

"I am reading the words of the sages."

"Are those sages alive?"

"They have died."

"Then, my liege, you are reading only the last dregs of the ancients."

"How could you, a wheelwright, have anything to say about what this royal person is reading? If you can explain yourself, I'll pardon you, but if you cannot, I shall have you beheaded!"

"Let your servant look at this from the viewpoint of his own job. If, when I make a wheel, I proceed too meekly, the wheel will not be strong. If I proceed too forcefully, the joints will not fit. Only when I am neither too meek nor too forceful will my hand express what's in my heart. Maybe this cannot be put fully into words, but there is still something to it. Your servant cannot give this insight to his son, nor can my son take it from me. That is why I am still carving wheels at the age of seventy. It's the same case as the words of those cultivated people: they are only the last dregs." (Z)

115 | The Frog in the Well

Have you heard of the frog in the ramshackle well and what it said to the gigantic turtle of the Eastern Sea?

"How happy I am," said the frog. "I can jump up the protruding bricks of the well. I can hop back down and linger on any brick I choose. Once I'm in the water, I stroke around with my head up. Or I dive to the muddy bottom and wiggle my feet. None of the crabs or tadpoles in the water can do any of this. I can claim this entire body of water as mine and have the greatest pleasure swimming and bobbing in this ramshackle well. Would you like to come in and try it yourself?"

But before the turtle of the Eastern Sea could even insert its left leg, its right knee got stuck, and he drew back.

The turtle then tried to tell the frog about his home in the Eastern Sea: "A distance of 5000 kilometers is not enough to describe how large it is. A measure of 20,000 meters is not enough to speak of its depth. In the time of Yu, there were nine floods within ten years, and yet the sea level never rose. During the time of Tang, there was drought eight years out of nine, but the headlands neither grew nor shrank. No events over any amount of time can alter the sea. It doesn't get larger or smaller; it doesn't advance or retreat. That is the great pleasure afforded by the Eastern Sea."

The frog was terrified and lost his composure. (Z)

116 | Dragging My Tail in the Mud

Zhuangzi was fishing on the banks of the Pu River when the King of Chu sent two envoys with this message: "I wish to trouble you with ruling the nation."

Zhuangzi held his rod steady and without turning around said: "I have heard that there is a divine tortoise shell in Chu and that the animal died three thousand years ago. The king stores this shell in a special wicker basket within his ancestral temple. Do you suppose it was better for the tortoise to die and have its shell venerated during grand ceremonies? Or would it have been better for it to live to drag its tail in the mud?"

"We suppose that it would have been better for it to have lived to drag its tail in the mud," answered the two envoys.

"Go then! I will drag my tail in the mud." (Z)

117 | The Phoenix and the Rat

When Hui Shi was prime minister of Liang, Zhuangzi traveled to visit him. While he was still on his way, someone told Hui Shi that Zhuangzi must have been coming to usurp him. Alarmed, Hui Shi ordered soldiers to scour the country for Zhuangzi. They searched for three days and three nights but could not find him. Zhuangzi arrived on his own, aware of what had happened, and said to Hui Shi:

"There is a bird in the south called the Young Firebird. Do you know it? It flies from the Southern Sea to the Northern Sea, never resting except in parasol trees, never eating anything except the fruit of the chinaberry, and never drinking anything except waters from the purest springs. When it passed an owl that was clutching a rotting rat, the owl looked up and tried to frighten the firebird off with a screech.

"Now, are you clutching the nation of Liang and screeching at me?" (Z)

118 | The Enjoyment of Fishes

Zhuangzi and Hui Shi were talking as they were crossing a bridge over the River Hao.

"When the fish come out and swim about at ease, that is what fish enjoy," said Zhuangzi.

"You are not a fish. How would you possibly know what fish enjoy?"

"You are not I. How do you know that I do not know what fish enjoy?"

"I may not be you, and I surely don't know you entirely, but you are definitely not a fish. That is my entire point that you could not possibly know what fish enjoy."

"Please go back to the original question. You asked how I knew what fish enjoyed. Well then, you must have already known that I knew when you asked me the question. I knew it by standing over the River Hao." (Z)

119 | Happiness

Under heaven, can perfect happiness be gotten or not? Are there any who can save themselves or not? Where are they now? What do they keep? Where do they avoid? Where do they stay? What do they pursue? What do they flee? What do they enjoy? What do they fear? (Z)

120 | What the World Honors

The world honors wealth, titles, longevity, and admiration. It delights in bodily comfort, rich flavors, pretty clothing, enthralling beauty, and pleasant music.

It deplores poverty, hardship, a short life, and illness. It views suffering as the body not getting enough rest and leisure, the mouth not tasting rich flavors, the figure not wearing perfect clothing, the eyes not seeing enthralling beauty, and the ears not hearing pleasant music. People are sad and afraid if they don't get these things.

All that for a body! How foolish! (Z)

121 | When Zhuangzi's Wife Died

Zhuangzi's wife died. Hui Shi went to pay his condolences, only to find Zhuangzi squatting on the ground, drumming on a brass basin, and singing.

"When a man's wife has lived with him, raised his children, and then dies in old age, that is overwhelming enough and he strains not to weep. Yet you beat a basin and sing! Isn't that excessive?"

"Not so," replied Zhuangzi. "When she first died, how could I not have been affected? But then I considered what she must have been before she had been born. She had no body before her birth, no movement, no shape, no breath. Then after some period of swirling, something changed and there was energy. Energy changed and there was form. Form changed and there was life. Now there has been another change and there is death. It's much the same as spring, summer, fall, and winter—the very sequence of the four seasons.

"Now she lies there as if sleeping in a great chamber. If I were to cry, shout, or wail, it would mean that I didn't understand life. So I refrain." (Z)

122 | When Heaven Initiates

The sages hide and store the power of heaven, and so nothing can harm them.

When dealing with an enemy, you would be careful not to break your sword. No matter how angry, you wouldn't take your rage out on a brick. In the same way, all under heaven could be peaceful and fair, free of the chaos of fighting and war, and without the punishments of executions and massacres if only we would all follow the same path.

People are not open to heaven, yet heaven and heaven alone has the power to initiate.

So for those people who aren't open to heaven, even while heaven and heaven alone has the power to initiate, let us remember: When heaven initiates, there is living virtue. When people take the initiative, there is living evil.

If we didn't reject heaven and we didn't neglect caring for other people, then who knows how many citizens might realize their true natures? (Z)

123 | Conversation with a Skull

Zhuangzi went to the state of Chu where he saw a skull by the side of the road. It had been bleached white, but it was still intact. He tapped it with his horsewhip.

"Sir, were you greedy in life? Did you make a mistake in reasoning? How did you reach this point? Did you lose in affairs of state? Were you beheaded by ax or halberd? How did you come to this?

"Did you do evil? Did you disgrace your parents, your wife, or your children? Did you suffer from cold and starvation? How did you come to this?

"Or did you simply reach the end of your springs and autumns?"

After asking these questions, Zhuangzi used the skull as a pillow and went to sleep.

That night, the skull appeared to him in a dream.

"You speak with scholarly eloquence. However, your observations and words are about the troubles of living people, whereas the dead don't have such problems. Would you like to hear about death?"

"I would," said Zhuangzi.

The skull said: "In death there is no ruler above and no minister below. There are none of the features of the four seasons, and yet we are with heaven and earth. Even the happiness of a king cannot surpass what we have."

Zhuangzi did not believe it, and asked, "If I asked the Ruler of Destiny to restore you to life with your bones, flesh, and skin, and to give you back your father and mother, your wife and children, and all your kin, would you want that?"

The skull glared at him. "Why should I reject supreme happiness and return to the toil of being a person again?" (Z)

124 | The Tumors

Uncle Zhi Li and Uncle Hua went to see the tomb of Uncle Ming in a hollow of the Kunlun Mountains. It was close to the Yellow Emperor's final resting place. Suddenly tumors appeared on their left elbows. Anyone would have thought that staggering and alarming.

Uncle Zhi Li turned to Uncle Hua: "Is this bad?"

"No," said Uncle Hua Jie. "Why should I think that this is bad? Life is borrowed. We're born to life temporarily—we're nothing but dust and dirt. Death and life are like day and night. You and I were just looking at the mound of one who has already gone through that change. If change is coming to me, why should I think that's bad?" (Z)

125 | The Drunk

The drunk falls off the cart and may get hurt, but he doesn't die. His bones and joints are the same as others, but his injuries are light. His spirit stays intact.

He didn't know he was riding on the cart, and he didn't know he fell off it. Anxiety over life and death isn't in him. So he encounters whatever may come without fear.

If he's that way when he's completely drunk, imagine what it would be like if he was completely with heaven! (Z)

126 | Confucius and the Hunchback

As Confucius was on his way to Chu, he passed through a forest and saw a hunchback catching cicadas with a sticky rod. "What is this?" Confucius asked. "Do you have Tao?"

"I do have some Tao," replied the hunchback. "For five or six months, I tried balancing two pellets on my rod without them falling. After I could do the same with three pellets, I only missed catching one cicada out of ten. Once I could balance five pellets without dropping them, I caught cicadas as if I were grabbing them with my hand.

"My body is like a broken stump; my arm is like a withered branch. Heaven and earth are great. The ten thousand things are many. Now I only notice cicada wings. I don't turn; I don't lunge. Nothing distracts me from the wings; how could I not succeed?"

Confucius turned to his students: "Use an undivided will and concentrate your spirits. That is what this venerable hunchback is telling you." (Z)

127 | The Ferryman

Yan Hui asked his teacher Confucius: "I was taking the ferry across the gulf of Shangshen. The ferryman steered the boat as if he was divine. I asked him, 'Can one learn to steer a boat like you?' He said, 'Yes. Good swimmers can learn it, and divers can learn right away without even seeing a boat.' But he wasn't any more specific than that. May I ask you what he meant?"

"Good swimmers can learn quickly," Confucius said, "because they don't worry about the water. As for good divers who learn without even seeing a boat, that's because they see a boat rocking on the gulf the same as being on a cart rolling down a slope. They've felt the movement of the water countless times, and they aren't disturbed by it.

"Archers vying to win a piece of pottery exert all their skill. Those trying to win a brass buckle grow nervous. And if the prize is gold, they shoot with dread. Their skill was the same in each case, but they became distracted by a sense of outer importance that led to internal crudeness." (Z)

128 | The Fighting Cocks

Ji Xingzi raised a fighting cock for the king. After ten days he was asked if the bird was ready, but he said, "Not yet. He is still immature and haughty and relies on his own power."

After another ten days, he was asked again, but he said, "Not yet. He is still distracted by his surroundings."

After another ten days, he was asked again, but he said, "Not yet. He still glares angrily and overflows with vigor."

After another ten days, he was asked again, but he said, "Almost. When another cock crows, he is unaffected. He looks as if he was made of wood. His qualities are complete. No other cock will dare to fight him, but will run from him instead." (Z)

129 | The Woodcarver

Qing the woodcarver was making a bell-stand, and when it was done, all who saw it thought it supernatural in quality. The Marquis of Lu went to see it and asked, "What artistry could produce this?"

"Your subject is just a workman," Qing replied. "How can I claim to have artistry? Nevertheless, there is one point. Before I, your subject, began work on the bell-stand, I conserved my breath. I fasted to still my mind. After fasting for three days, I did not venture to think of praise, reward, rank, or satisfaction. After fasting for five days, I did not dare to think of rejection, skill, or convention. After fasting for seven days, I had forgotten myself, my four limbs and my entire person. By this time, even any thought of your court was gone. Everything that could interfere with my skill vanished.

"Only then did I go into the mountain forests, observing the natural forms of trees. When I found the perfect one, I could already see the bell-stand in it, and only then did I apply my hands. If I had not found the right tree, I would have given up. But when conditions are in accord with heaven, the spirit is unerring and so the bell-stand was assured. How could it be otherwise?" (Z)

130 | How to Nurture a Bird

A bird happened to alight from the wilds and walked into the palace. The King of Lu was so pleased that he provided a banquet to which he brought an ox, a sheep, and a pig, and he ordered the Nine Songs of Emperor Shun to be performed.

The bird only dipped its head, looked forlorn and confused, and did not dare drink or eat. This is called "treating a bird as you would treat yourself."

If you would nurture a bird, nurture it as a bird should be nurtured. Leave it to roost in a deep forest, drift on rivers and lakes, and find its own worms. Leave it to find its own way on flat ground. (Z)

131 | True Benevolence

Every new year's day, the people of Handan presented live doves to Governor Jian. This delighted him and he rewarded the donors lavishly.

A visitor asked the meaning of the custom, and Governor Jian explained that the release of living creatures on new year's day was an act of mercy.

The visitor replied: "The people know that your majesty loves this ceremony of liberation. They vie with one another to catch as many doves as possible, and many birds are accidentally killed in the process. If you want to affirm life, tell the people that you no longer want them to catch doves for you, and you will have no need to grant mercy." (L)

132 | An Ugly Woman Imitates a Beauty

When the great beauty Xi Shi got upset, she glared at everyone in her village. An ugly woman saw how beautiful Xi Shi was and tried to imitate the same glaring expression.

When the wealthy people of the village saw her, they barred their doors and refused to come out. When the poor men saw her, they grabbed their wives and children and ran away.

The woman saw that a glaring woman was beautiful, but she did not realize that it wasn't the glaring that made the woman beautiful. (Z)

133 | Only Seeing Gold

In the state of Qi during ancient times, there was a man who had a burning lust for gold. Rising early one morning, he got dressed, put on his hat and went to the marketplace. He walked into a money-changer's shop, grabbed all the gold he could, and ran off.

The magistrate's men caught him and asked why he was doing this: "There are people everywhere. How did you think you could snatch all that gold?"

"When I took the gold, I did not look at anyone. I only looked at the gold." (L)

134 | Suspicion

A man lost his ax and suspected that his neighbor's son had taken it. He watched the way that the boy walked—he moved just like someone who would steal an ax. He examined the boy's demeanor—he looked just like someone who would steal an ax. He listened to his talk—he spoke just like someone who would steal an ax. In his actions, movements, and his bearing, it was plain that he had stolen the ax.

Sometime later, the man was digging in a dell and came across his missing ax.

The next day, when he saw the neighbor's son again, he found that his actions, movement, and bearing did not seem at all like someone who would steal an ax. (L)

135 | Clever Writing

A man named Zhang once stole three hundred ounces of silver. That night, he buried the bundle beneath a wall. Afraid that someone else would look for it, he posted a sign that read: "There are not three hundred ounces of silver buried here."

But his neighbor, a man named Wang, had seen Zhang digging in the night. So he went to the spot later and found the silver. Afraid that Zhang would suspect that he had taken the treasure, Wang thought himself clever to leave his own note: "Your neighbor Wang did not steal your silver." (FT)

136 | Spear and Shield

A man went to the marketplace to sell shields and spears. He called for people to gather around him.

First he raised a shield. "My shields are so strong that no spear can pierce them!"

Then he gripped a spear. "My spears are so sharp that nothing can stop them!"

A bystander called out: "What if one of your spears was used to strike one of your shields?"

The seller could give no answer. (HFZ)

137 | On Usefulness and Uselessness

Zhuangzi was walking in the mountains with his disciples when he saw a tall tree with thick branches and lush foliage. A woodcutter holding an ax stood nearby but didn't move to chop it down, and when he was asked why, he said that the tree was useless.

"Since this tree has no useful qualities, it will live out its natural life," Zhuangzi said.

When Zhuangzi left the mountain, he went to stay at the house of an old friend who was overjoyed to see him. He ordered his servant-boy to kill a goose and boil it to serve their guest. The boy asked: "One of our geese can honk, but the other one can't. Which one shall I kill?"

The master of the house said, "The one that can't honk."

The next day, one of Zhuangzi's disciples said: "Yesterday you said that the tree on the mountain would live out its natural life because it was useless. But a goose was killed because it was deemed useless. Which of these cases should we follow?"

"Most of the time, it would seem that having qualities is better than having no qualities," Zhuangzi laughed. "But if it was a matter of choosing between having qualities and having none, I would choose none because I could then avoid all sorts of trouble. I would much rather rely on drifting and floating upon the abundant Tao." (Z)

183

138 | Waiting for a Hare to Appear

Long ago, a farmer in the state of Song was plowing his fields when a running hare rammed into a tree trunk, breaking its neck and falling dead. The farmer got the hare without any effort.

After that, the farmer abandoned his plow to wait for the next hare to come along. But another one never ran into the tree again. (HFZ)

139 | Knowledge and Nonaction

Knowledge was traveling in the north near Dark Water where he climbed the Slope of the Hidden. There he encountered Mute Nonaction. Knowledge said: "I would like to ask you some questions. What thought and pondering lead us to Tao? Where can we go and what can we do to be safe in Tao? What method could we follow to reach Tao?" Mute Nonaction did not reply to Knowledge's questions. Not only did he not speak—he didn't know what to answer.

Unable to get any answers, Knowledge returned south to White Water, where he climbed the Slope of Fox Heights. There he met Crooked Crazy. He put the same three questions to him.

"Ah! I know," said Crooked Crazy. But just as he was about to speak, he forgot what he wanted to say.

Again receiving no answers to his questions, Knowledge went to the palace, and he asked the Yellow Emperor the same three questions.

The emperor said: "Only when there is no thought and no pondering is there Tao. Only when we go nowhere and do nothing are we safe in Tao. Only when we follow no method can we reach Tao." (Z)

185

140 | Talking at the Right Level

Confucius paused during his travels when his horse got loose and began eating someone else's oats. A rough local man captured the horse.

Zigong, one of the Confucius's disciples, asked for permission to ask the man to return the horse and Confucius agreed. But Zigong's language was so lofty that the man could not understand him.

There was a lowly man who had just begun studying with Confucius and who volunteered to try. He went up to the man and said, "Sir, you plow from the Eastern Sea to the Western Sea, so how could our horse not eat your oats?"

The man was pleased. "All talk should be as logical as yours! How could anyone be as dense as that other fellow?" He released the horse.

If ways of speaking like this cannot be compared, then how can outside things be decided?

When it comes to personal conduct, the cultivated person respects others without worrying about getting respect in return and loves others without expecting love in return.

Respect and love depend on oneself. Whether respect and love are returned depends on others. The cultivated person knows what is within but cannot be sure of others. To be certain of what is within oneself is to be prepared for all encounters. (LBW)

141 | You Can't Possess Tao

Shun asked Cheng: "Can one possess Tao?"

"Your body is not yours to have," answered Cheng. "How then could you possess Tao?"

"If you say that my body is not mine to possess, then who possesses it?"

"Heaven and earth entrusted your body to you, and life is not yours to possess. It is yours because of heaven and earth. Neither your nature nor your life are yours to own.

"Just as heaven and earth appointed you and just as you must go along with that, your grandsons and sons are also not yours to possess. In sum, heaven and earth appointed all your offspring.

"Therefore, when we walk, we do not have to worry about where we're going. Wherever we live, we do not have to think of support. When we eat, we don't have to worry about taste. Heaven and earth are overwhelmingly powerful—so how could you possess Tao?" (Z)

142 | Where Is Tao?

Dongguo Zi asked Zhuangzi: "Where is Tao found?"

"Everywhere."

"Can you be specific?"

"It's in an ant."

"Can you be more basic than that?"

"It's in the weeds."

"Can you be even more basic than that?"

"It's in a clay tile."

"Can you be still more basic than that?"

"It's in shit."

Dongguo Zi was silent. (Z)

143 | Fame

Yang Zhu said: "You may do good without thinking about fame, but fame will follow. Fame may come with no thought of gain, but gain will return. Gain may be made with no thought of strife, but strife will always appear. Thus the cultivated person is careful when doing good." (L)

144 | On Tao

On Tao: it can be felt and trusted, but it moves on its own and it has no form.

It can be given but not taken. It can be summoned but not kept. It is its own origin and root. It came before heaven and earth. It is ancient and imbues everything, including gods, ghosts, spirits, and kings.

It birthed heaven. It birthed earth. It is higher than the highest of the greatest extremes. It is lower than the lowest of lowest extremes. Indeed, it came before heaven and earth and before there was time. It goes back long before the greatest antiquity, and yet it can never be called worn or old. (Z)

Sources

(BD)   *Book of Documents*
(BR)   *Book of Rites*
(CMS)   *Classic of Mountains and Seas*
(CP)   *Classic of Poetry*
(FT)   folktale
(FL)   *The Forest of Laughter*
(HFZ)   *Han Fei Zi*
(L)   *Liezi*
(LBW)   *The Spring and Autumn of Lu Buwei*
(RH)   *Records of the Grand Historian*
(TYM)   Essay by Tao Yuanming and a folktale
(YJ)   *Yijing (I Ching)*
(Z)   *Zhuangzi*

Hampton Roads Publishing Company
. . . for the evolving human spirit

Hampton Roads Publishing Company publishes books
on a variety of subjects, including spirituality, health,
and other related topics.

For a copy of our latest trade catalog, call (978) 465-0504
or visit our distributor's website at *www.redwheelweiser.com*. You can
also sign up for our newsletter and special offers by going to
www.redwheelweiser.com/newsletter/.